THE ANNUAL REVIEW OF
W O M E N
IN
WORLD RELIGIONS
VOLUME I

The editors of *Women in World Religions* welcome articles, books for review, book reviews, and suggestions. Major articles should be between 20 and 30 typed, double-spaced pages (5000 to 7530 words) in length, including notes, appendices, and bibliography. Articles should have endnotes (not footnotes). In addition to the hard copy, diskettes should also be submitted whenever possible. Ideally they should be double side/double density and Word-Perfect 5.1 (though other programs can be converted here). Standards of documentation and style should conform to Walter S. Achtert and Joseph Gibaldi, *The MLA Style Manual* (New York: Modern Language Association of America, 1985). The use of the author-date system of internal references, with full bibliographic data at the end of the article, is recommended. The conventions of American spelling should be followed. An abstract of no more than 500 words should accompany the article, and a brief *curriculum vitae* of the author should be enclosed.

Submissions should be addressed to:

The Editors
Women in World Religions
Faculty of Religious Studies
McGill University
3520 University Street
Montreal, Quebec
Canada H3A 2A7

THE ANNUAL REVIEW OF
W O M E N
IN
WORLD RELIGIONS
VOLUME I

Edited by
Arvind Sharma
and
Katherine K. Young

State University of New York Press

Published by
State University of New York Press, Albany

For information, address State University of New York Press,
State University Plaza, Albany, N.Y. 12246

The Annual review of women in world religions
ISSN 1056-4578

ISBN 0-7914-0865-5

ISBN 0-7914-0866-3 (pbk.)

10 9 8 7 6 5 4 3 2 1

EDITORIAL

A book entitled: *Women in World Religions* was published by the SUNY Press in 1987. The reception indicated that it met a felt need. It also seemed to vindicate the historical and phenomenological approach to the study of women in world religions. The relevance of both subject and method seemed to call for an ongoing forum to contine discussing themes covered in the book. We therefore decided, with the cooperation of the SUNY Press, to launch a journal providing such a forum.

This journal will appear as an annual. Due to the common ground it shares with the book mentioned above, of which it is a lineal descendant, we have decided to call it *The Annual Review of Women in World Religions*.

This *Annual Review of Women in World Religions* has been conceived as polymethodic, interdisciplinary and multi-traditional in its approach to the study of women and religion. It will not only allow the comparative dimension to appear in bolder relief, but will also help establish a dialogue between the two solitudes of humanistic and social scientific studies in the field. We hope that it will be welcomed in academic circles.

Arvind Sharma   Katherine K. Young

THE ANNUAL REVIEW OF WOMEN IN WORLD RELIGIONS

EXECUTIVE EDITORS

Arvind Sharma   Katherine K. Young

EDITORIAL BOARD

CONTENTS

Mary Gerhart
Another Troy for Her to Burn: The True Story
of Euripides' Helen 1

Denyse Rockey
Three Faces of The Great Goddess:
Shulamite, Cinderella, Black Virgin 31

Winnie Tomm
Goddess Consciousness and Social Realities:
The 'Permeable Self' 71

Katherine K. Young
Goddesses, Feminists, and Scholars 105

ANOTHER TROY FOR HER TO BURN
THE TRUE STORY OF EURIPIDES' HELEN

Mary Gerhart

Research on goddesses of ancient times has been most firmly based on statues of mother goddess figures, inscriptions, hymns, and heroic tales of women gods. Research on women of ancient times proceeds on the basis of artistic iconography, necrology, ethnography, and history. And while we have been cautioned not to take literally the descriptions and prohibitions recorded in either image or language, scholarly studies nevertheless have too often made empirical facts out of the evidence (such as Eva C. Keuls' *The Reign of the Phallus: Sexual Politics in Ancient Athens* [1985]). Others have concentrated on the symbolic significance of the figures for psychological insight and inspiration (e.g., Chris Downing's *The Goddess* [1981]). Although the results of these approaches have been productive — they have peopled our past with images of women hitherto obscured, distorted or ignored in androcentric history — the religious significance of "goddess" for theology in general is still in question.[1]

The myths of Helen are a valuable and challenging resource for understanding the goddess since no fewer than three major variations on the myth were known in ancient times. Only two of the three versions appear in the extant plays of Euripides. By asking why the fertility goddess version does not appear in the plays of this author, we may re-map an understanding of the goddess for our time. But how shall we proceed in the face of three different versions of the Helen story? What is the true story of Helen?

We have learned from Paul Ricoeur that the first task is to listen again to the myths. Myths have not been made obsolete by the specialization of though in philosophy and theology. By reflection on the multiple avowals of experience represented in myths, the philosopher is forestalled from any premature closure on questions that require more than logical answers. For Ricoeur, a good philosophical interpretation of narrative is one that accounts for the greatest number of perceived details in the narrative and that does so at the highest level of persuasion. Regarding what is to be perceived, we have learned from Julia Kristeva to observe in what ways the language of myth is doubly bound: bound to the human body and its desires and bound to the body politic and its structures.[2] Kristeva's work in literary and in psychoanalytic theory is particularly apt for a retrieval of Helen from selective memory. In addition, Kristeva's work is helpful in addressing the question of the religious significance of the goddess today.[3]

* * * * * * * * * * *

Once upon a time there was a beautiful woman, born the daughter of Leda of Sparta and Zeus. While still a young girl, she was abducted to Athens by Theseus and Polydeuces. Because the Athenians were aghast at what Theseus had done, he sent Helen away to his mother for safekeeping. After bearing a daughter, Helen was rescued by her brothers, Castor and Pollux. When she grew up, many heroes and chieftains of all Greece made suit for her in marriage, and her foster father, Tyndareus, was frightened out of his wits by the possibility that the unsuccessful suitors would attack him. He thought up the ingenious solution that each suitor had to promise to defend her husband — i.e., the one who finally won Helen's hand — if any harm came to him. With or without her consent (we don't know), Menelaus became her husband and heir to the throne.

Meanwhile Paris awarded Aphrodite the golden apple which Eris had tossed among the wedding guests at the marriage of Peleus and Thetis, and in return won Helen, said to be the most beautiful woman in the world.[4] The snag was that she was already married. No matter — in the spirit of ancient times, Paris, with his father Priam's consent, set off for Greece where he was courteously entertained by Menelaus. When Menelaus went to Crete for his grandfather's funeral, Paris abducted Helen.

Here the story breaks into two versions. In Version One, Paris took Helen and married her in Troy, where she bore several children, all of whom died in infancy. In the first version, the Trojan women are divided up among the Greek victors after the War, and Menelaus grudgingly takes Helen back. In Version Two, recorded for the first time by Stesichorus (a sixth century BCE poet who, according to C.M. Bowra,[5] had to placate those of his contemporaries who regarded Helen as a goddess), Helen never went to Troy, having been spirited away to Egypt for the twenty years of the War and its aftermath. There are variations on each of these two versions as well.

Euripides was not the only classical writer to refer to both of the two major versions of the legend. According to Herodotus, Homer must have known both versions but did not find the Helen-in-Egypt version amenable to the demands of epic narrative.[6] Herodotus further argued for the "truth" of the Helen-in-Egypt version (Version Two) on the supposition that, had Helen been in Troy (according to Version One), the Trojans would surely have surrendered her rather than have their city destroyed. Herodotus therefore believed the Trojans were speaking truly when they said that Helen was not there.

An older myth, which we will refer to as Version Three, predates both the foregoing epic versions of the myth of Helen and the dramatic versions that we will consider shortly. From the third century BCE poet Theocritus and the first century CE geographer Pausanias, we know that before the Homeric epic Helen was originally a nature goddess of fertility and that she had been worshipped in Sparta, Rhodes, and other cities.[7] Both the fertility goddess legend and Helen's lineage as specified in the epic myths certify that she was godly.

Whether Euripides suppressed this oldest version of Helen or whether it was not known to him, we find no trace of it in the extant Euripidean plays, believed to be a third of all he wrote. Version One is frequently employed alone; Version Two is always presented over and against Version One.

If Euripides did know about this archaic tradition of Helen as a goddess of fertility, why did he not draw upon this Third Version of the myth? First, it has been noticed that when Euripides wrote about heroes and stories of the Trojan War, he selected events which either preceded or followed the War as it was narrated in *The Iliad* and *The Odyssey*. *Rhesus* (440), his first play, which takes material directly from *The Iliad*, is the only exception. Since the older myth of Helen is neither in the epics as narrated by Homer nor related explicitly to the War, it is consistent for Euripides not to include a reference to Helen's earliest appearance in Greek culture. Second, gods and goddesses function integrally in the plots of Euripides' plays, often in direct relation to the psychological aspects of human characters. Thus, Dionysus in *The Bacchae* and Aphrodite and Artemis in *Hippolytus* both reflect and affect the action of the plays. Conception and birth in the Euripidean plays, however, are usually attributed to the action — frequently the violent action — of gods. Creusa in *Ion*, for example, comes to the Oracle at Delphi to petition for a child to replace the one she had borne by Zeus and abandoned. On the way into the temple, she wonders where women can find justice when power belongs to the unjust, perhaps alluding to the overbearing androcentrism of Greek religion. And when the Chorus in *Helen* connects Helen to Demeter, goddess of fertility, and to Persephone, goddess of death, we may speak of a vicarious identification of Helen with fertility goddess.[8]   Yet this analogue is only an oblique reference to Version Three of the Helen myth.   Must we conclude that Euripides was incapable of dramatizing a fertility goddess who also acted in history?

I. Helen as Portrayed in Euripides: Receiving the Tradition

Of the twenty extant complete plays[9] of Euripides, Helen is referred to by name in ten of the plays, she is among the cast of characters in two of the plays (*Orestes* and *The Trojan Women*), and in *Helen* she is the main character and subject. These references span the corpus of Euripides, with the first in *Rhesus*, his first play (440 BCE) and the last in *Iphigenia in Aulis* (405 BCE), which with *The Bacchae*, was produced posthumously.

Table I: *Citations to Helen in Euripides' plays* (citations in the play *Helen*, where she appears as the main character, were not counted)

Title of Play	Year Produced	Number of Citations
Rhesus	(440)	1
*Alcestis**	(438)	0
*Medea**	(431)	0
Heracleidae	(429)	0
*Hippolytus**	(428)	0
Cyclops	(425)	2
Hecuba	(425)	5
Phoenix	(425)	0

Table I (continued)

Title of Play	Year Produced	Number of Citations
Heracles	(424-420)	0
The Suppliant Women	(420-415)	0
Andromache	(419)	5
*The Trojan Women**	(415)	7
Iphigenia in Tauris	(414-410)	5
Electra	(413)	6
Helen*	(412)	multiple
Ion	(411)	0
*Phoenician Women**	(411-409)	0
*Orestes**	(408)	29
*Iphigenia in Aulis**	(405)	15
*The Bacchae**	(405)	0

Chronologically, the plays fall roughly into four groups with respect to Euripides' treatment of Helen. Of the first ten of the extant plays, written or produced between 440 and 420, references to Version One of Helen appear in only three of the plays (*Rhesus, Hecuba,* and *The Cyclops*). Of the next four extant plays, written or produced between 419 and 413, Version One of Helen is referred to in all four plays (*Andromache, The Trojan Women, Iphigenia in Tauris,* and *Electra*). In *Electra*, Version Two of the Helen myth is introduced as a playbill in the closing lines. Of the last five extant plays, written or produced between 412 and 405, one play (*Helen*) elaborated Version Two of Helen over and against Version One. Of the last three plays (*Orestes, Iphigenia in Aulis,* and *The Bacchae*), two together have more references (Version One or, in *Orestes,* a modification thereof) to Helen than all of the previous plays, excluding *Helen.*

(*plays whose dates are confidently set by ancient testimony)[10]

The plays also document an increasing complexity in the character of Helen, both in terms of her relations to characters speaking of her and in terms of her function in the total action of the plays.

In the following quotations, taken from the three earliest plays in the above list, the references to Helen are uniformly derogatory. In *Rhesus*, the Chorus of Trojan guards pray that Dolon, one of their warriors, who plans to crawl by night as a spy in the disguise of a wolf to the Greek ships, will kill one of the Greeks:

Chorus of Trojan guards: Might it be Menelaus!
                              Or might he kill Agamemnon
                              and bring the head back as
                              a gloomy gift for the arms of his
                              evil sister by marriage, Helen...
                              (ll. 259-60)

In *The Cyclops*, a racy exchange is the context for the first reference to Helen:

Coryphaeus: Did you take Helen when you took Troy?
Odysseus: We rooted out the whole race of Priam.
Coryphaeus: When you took that woman, did you all take
              turns and bang her? She liked variety in men,
              the fickle bitch! Why, the sight of a man
              with embroidered pants and a golden chain
              so fluttered her, she left Menelaus,
              a fine little man. I wish there were
              no women in the world — except for me.
              (177-86)

This bawdy humor, irony that is characteristic of the satyr-play, nevertheless raises the gender issue explicitly and alludes to

Helen as the cause of the war. The other reference to Helen in *The Cyclops* is simply to "that foul Helen" who was carried off.

In *Hecuba*, the Trojan queen, Hecuba, has ample reason to hate Helen. She has lost her daughter, Polyxena (sacrificed for the ghost of Achilles), her other daughter, Cassandra (taken as slave to Agamemnon), and her grandson, Astyanax (slaughtered by a traitor to their family) — all, she thinks, because of Helen:

Hecuba: Whoever hurt him [Achilles] less
               than this poor girl [Polyxena]? If death is what
               he wants, let Helen die. He went to Troy for
               her; for *her* he died. (265-66)

Yet Hecuba acknowledges Helen's beauty as well, and for the first time in Euripides — albeit ironically — something nice is said about Helen. If the ghost of Achilles requires "dying loveliness" to appease his hurt,

Hecuba: Look to Helen,
               loveliest of lovely women on this earth
               by far — lovely Helen, who did him harm
               far more than we. (268-70)

The Chorus of Trojan women also curse Helen:

Chorus of Trojan women: Helen, fury of ruin!
                           Let the wind blow
                           and never bring her home!
                           Let there be no landing
                           for Helen of Troy! (950-954)

In another passage, however, the Chorus pushes the blame back to Paris' action and praises Helen's beauty:

Chorus of Trojan women: That morning was my fate,
that hour doom was done,
when Paris felled the tree
that grew on Ida's height
and made a ship for sea
and sailed to Helen's bed —

loveliest of women
the golden sun has seen. (629-637)

Helen appears as a character for the first time in *The Trojan Women*. In her own defense, she speaks (albeit unconvincingly) of the strength of the goddess who pressures her to go with Paris.

In this first group of plays, therefore, Euripides does not stray from one-dimensional understandings of Helen. He does not go beyond the broadest strokes of Version One of the received myths of his time. The only complexity is that portrayed through the figure of Hecuba who nevertheless repeats the conventional understandings of Helen.

The plays of the middle group continue to blame Helen for the Trojan War and praise her beauty as well as introduce more complex attitudes. In *Andromache*, for example, Menelaus uses empathy to defend his rescue of Andromache:

Menelaus: Let's just suppose your daughter
Married some citizen and got such treatment,
You'd sit back mum? I doubt it....
When cheated, wife or husband feels the same.
She doesn't like it. He doesn't either,
... Yet he can mend things with his good right arm;
She has to count on friends' or parents' aid.

Menelaus' sympathy for Helen is colored by his own opportunism as well:

Menelaus: Poor Helen had a time of it, not choosing
             But chosen by the gods to exalt her country.
             For innocent before of arms and battles
             Greece grew to manhood then. Experience,
             travel —
             These are an education in themselves.
             If coming in the presence of my wife

             I steeled myself and spared her, I was wise.
             (ll. 668-86)

Given the wimpy character of Menelaus in this play, it may be too strong to interpret the foregoing lines as evidence of Euripides' critical reflection on gender issues. Nevertheless, four years later, in *The Trojan Women*, for the first time in Euripidean drama, the Greeks in general, rather than Paris or Helen, are blamed for the War. Cassandra (Hecuba's daughter) makes no mention of a political basis for the Greeks' pursuit of Helen: the motive, she says, was "an act of love":

Cassandra: For one woman's sake,
              one act of love, these [Achaeans] hunted Helen
              down and threw thousands of lives away.
              (367-69)

This criticism of the Greeks is overshadowed in the next line by Helen's being referred to as a "vile woman" and later being blamed by Hecuba for having "brought to ruin all our house" (1215). In this play, nevertheless, Helen appears as a character for the first time and, by anticipating the charges that Menelaus will bring against her, speaks for herself in a three-fold argument: (1) It is more appropriate to blame the mother of

Paris (Hecuba) than Helen herself for the Trojan War; (2) Helen's misfortune in winning the beauty contest had the good effect of the Greeks' being free from Asia's domination; (3) It was a strong goddess who intervened twice on behalf of taking and keeping Helen in Troy. Helen's argument is reasonable even though it is effectively countered by Hecuba, and Helen's being treated as a slave along with the Trojan Women generates some sympathy for her as a character, especially in contrast with Hecuba and Menelaus, who become progressively less admirable.

In *Iphigenia in Tauris*, Menelaus and Helen are together blamed by Iphigenia for having caused her to be sacrificed by her father, Agamemnon. Unmitigated hatred of Helen by Iphigenia here and by Electra in the next play (*Electra*) continues with little variation. The one exception occurs as a kind of play-bill announcement at the end of *Electra* that introduces Version Two, the Helen-in-Egypt story. Menelaus, having just come home from the Trojan War, will bury his sister-in-law, Clytemnestra, freshly murdered by Orestes and Electra. Castor, one of Helen's brothers (the Dioscuri), at the end of the play pronounces:

Castor: Helen will help him. She never went to Troy.
                 Zeus fashioned and dispatched a Helen-image there
                 to Ilium so men might die in hate and blood.
                 (1280-1283)

Thus we see that when Euripides finally introduced Version Two, he did so at privileged points in the dramatic action: at the end of *Electra* and the beginning of *Helen*. In the Prologue to *Helen*, the character Helen states:

Helen: Thus, though I wear the name of guilt in Greece,
                yet here I keep my body uncontaminated by
                disgrace. (66-67)

There are many reasons to read *Helen* as a serious play. Yet
the play has usually been read as a farce. One wonders if the
discrepancy between Versions One and Two of the Helen myth,
a discrepancy explicit in the play, had anything to do with
assigning the play to the genre of farce, an assignment which
prevents the play from being taken seriously. A few scholars
have read *Helen* as a romantic comedy — an interpretation more
able to account for more elements of the plot than is farce.
What all commentators have overlooked, however, is that the
play is also epistemologically interesting in that it raises
questions about what constitutes identity and how we know what
we claim to know about others. Version One of the myth is
alluded to only to be discredited in the unfolding of new events.
Interpretation is explicitly called for. Teucer says of Tyndareus'
sons (Helen's brothers): "[They are] dead, not dead, / There are
two interpretations here" (ll. 138-39). Also unique to this play
is the reunion scene between Helen and Menelaus:

Menelaus: I see it, I see it! All the story that she told
               has come out true. O day of my desires, that
               gave you back into my arms to take and hold
               again!....

               Helen: I am so happy, all my hair is rising
               with shivering pleasure, and the tears burst.
               Husband and love, I have your body here close
               in my arms, happiness, mine again.
               (623-25, 632-35).

Finally, the play *Helen* elaborates on the futility of the war, and
raises questions about the mixed motives of the Greeks. *Helen*

requires a new reading in an age alert to androcentric distortions. For our purposes, however, the change in the portrayal of Helen can be taken as a key issue in determining more comprehensively who Helen is.

In *Orestes*, written about a year before Euripides voluntarily exiled himself to Macedon, the action begins where *Electra* left off (before the reference to Version Two of the myth): with Helen returning to Argos from Troy with Menelaus to bury Clytemnestra. Orestes and Pylades plot to kill Helen and to kill her daughter, Hermione, ostensibly to hurt Menelaus who has refused their request for an army to wage war for Orestes' release and their safe passage from the country. Apollo rescues Helen from their deadly attack and announces:

Apollo: Helen lives,
                 for being born of Zeus, she could not die,
                 and now, between the Dioscuri in the swathe
                 of air, she sits enthroned forever, a star
                 for sailors. (1634-1637)

In a passage which could be interpreted either as a radically unbelievable solution for a hopeless situation or as a symbolic statement of desire for a new beginning, Apollo decrees that

Apollo: Menelaus must marry again,
                 since the gods by means of Helen's loveliness
                 drove Trojans and Greeks together in war
                 and made them die, that [e]arth might be
                 lightened
                 of her heavy burden of mortality. (1638-1642)

A few lines later, Menelaus is further instructed to take the kingship of Sparta, ostensibly because it was "the dowry of

Helen, whose only dowry yet has been your anguish and suffering" (1661-1663).

In the last play which mentions Helen (*Iphigenia in Aulis*), performed posthumously, Menelaus is his typical self, arguing with Agamemnon that killing Iphigenia is not worth doing "to gain a Helen" (468). Euripides reverts to Version One of the myth to portray a psychoanalytically fascinating appropriation of guilt by Iphigenia, who is the prime victim of the affair. Beside the usual appellations of "wicked Helen," there is the despair of Iphigenia as she asks,

Iphigenia: Oh, oh — the marriage
              of Paris and Helen — Why must it touch
              my life? Why must Paris be my ruin?
              (1236-1238)

More poignant is Iphigenia's willingness to give her life as expiation for the destructive situation:

Iphigenia: ... Because of me, never more will
              Barbarians wrong and ravish Greek women,
              drag them from happiness and their homes
              in Hellas. The penalty will be paid
              fully for the shame and seizure of Helen.
              (1379-1382)

Iphigenia appropriates the responsibility formerly attributed completely to Helen, Paris, or the Greeks. With this displacement of responsibility, Euripides has moved from myth as origin, to myth as referent to the present and vector for a future.

II. Interpreting the Variance among the Figures of Helen

Among the different figures of Helen from all three versions of the myth, is there an interpretation that will take all three into account?   Julia Kristeva provides some leading threads[11] for our task of putting together a coherent identity for Helen.

In Kristeva's theory, the speaking subject is characterized by two modes in relation to her place in the system of language. These modes correspond to two correlative roles, which, she thinks, are exercised simultaneously: (1) the symbolic role by which the speaking subject advances the prevailing public texts and systems of representation, and (2) the semiotic role by which the speaking subject transgresses, ruptures, and transforms the prevailing systems of meaning and representation. For Kristeva, the symbolic is hierarchically regulated and subordinated to "phallic sexuality."   The semiotic refers to manifestations of libido and bodily energies, as well as to certain texts which resist replacement by the symbolic order of speech. Most immediately, the semiotic refers to "pre-Oedipal primary processes" experienced as basic pulsions or forces ("chorae") which flow in ceaseless articulations across the body. Some articulations are dichotomous (e.g., life vs. death, pleasure vs. pain); others are heterogeneous (e.g., guilt, shame, fear). Language, in Kristeva's view, is a dialectic between the symbolic (the totality of conventional meanings at any given time) and the semiotic.

For our purposes, it is helpful to think of the collection of images of Helen as she is represented in Euripides as both semiotic and symbolic: symbolic in the sense that the meanings associated with the three versions of the Helen myth have in fact been understood dichotomously (Helen is by turns evil and beneficent, bringer of bad fate and initiator of rescue, human and goddess) and have been reduced to two characteristics (worthy of praise, worthy of blame) related by the genital principle; semiotic in the sense that the broad range of her portrayed characteristics resists translation into any simple proposition. What is most remembered about Helen, a memory reinforced by the sparse images of Helen in the early plays, is her beauty *and* her blame in causing the Trojan War and all the evil visited upon both the Greeks and the Trojans.

That the symbolic realm of the Greeks is dominated by the phallic principle is not news to us. That the androcentrically initiated Trojan War was only one of a series of rape/ abductions of noble women and goddesses we know well from Herodotus.[12] Kristeva helps us to locate and to understand better the internal resistance to patriarchal domination — resistance such as that experienced in reading Euripides' plays. This resistance surpasses a mere surmise about the author's "attitude," such as crediting Euripides with being either a genius or a misogynist with respect to his portrayal of women. We need not attribute the resistance to patriarchal domination found in the plays to the genius of Euripides alone but can understand that resistance more importantly as a tension operating from within the self-identity of the Greeks — a tension between a semiotic realm of paradox, contradiction, *jouissance*, shifting identities and a symbolic order of unreflective genitality. We have already seen evidence that the story of Helen figured prominently in the self-identity of the Greeks. In *Andromache*, for example, we saw Menelaus crediting Helen with the "exultation" of Greece: in the experience of war, he thought, "Greece grew to manhood then" (11. 668-672). In this sense, the story of Helen and the Trojan War functions as a second genesis for the Greeks, a frequently interpreted founding story which referred back to the time when the present became what it was. Kristeva's theory of how meaning and significance come into being makes it possible to reflect on the complete inventory of references and appearances of Helen in Euripides with an expectation that they are significant, not only within the context of each play and not only in summary, but also as they jockey for position among themselves and in the reader's world of meanings.

On the one hand, we are prevented from reducing the meaning of Helen to beauty and blame or to any easy way of relating these two major themes, even in Euripides' early work. We must attend to figures other than Helen, who are blamed as the cause of the Trojan War for example, Paris or the gods and goddesses (see *The Trojan Women*, 920-26). Rather than assign any essential meaning to beauty and to blame, we are encouraged by Kristeva's theory to see these two strands of meaning in an uneasy relationship with other strands of meaning which conspire to define who the Greeks were.

As a result of Kristeva's theory, we are also encouraged to look for contradictions and interruptions of meaning as an internal critique of the symbolic order. Many nineteenth- and twentieth-century readers of Euripides have been reductionist in the sense that they read in his work only decline and secularization of belief in the gods and goddesses. But while Euripides' treatment of gods and goddesses is decidedly different from that of Aeschylus or of Sophocles, the ambiguity which characterizes Euripides' treatment of the gods deserves more than a swift dismissal. Indeed, within this dismissal there remains to be explored some critics' odd elevation of "true" (read "simple" and "unquestioning") belief which they say is to be found in Euripides' precursors, against the critics' approbation of what they call Euripides' secularization of religion. With Kristeva's theory, these reductive interpretations (e.g., Euripides no longer believes in gods and goddesses; Euripides challenges the existence of the gods) can be seen to eliminate what is ultimately most valuable in understanding the plays.[13] For with Kristeva's theory, as one explicator of her work wrote, "the acceptance of negativity or the fading of meaning can lead to the emergence of a new positivity of meaning" and "the only positivity presently acceptable involves the multiplication of languages, logics and powers."[14] For Kristeva, this multiplicity includes language, rhetoric and literature as "terrains of an accepted madness."[15] We could add to this list of terrains certain aspects of religion as well.

We are now prepared to retrieve the goddess image of Helen according to a religious logic. We have seen that in one of Euripides' last references to Helen, Helen is restored, albeit miraculously by Zeus, to goddess status, by which she "sits enthroned forever, a star for sailors" (*Orestes*, ll. 1637-38). Her restoration was foretold in *Helen* where the action is initiated by a trio of women and both Helen and Menelaus are promised divine status after they return to Greece where their lives eventually end. Euripides' restoration of Helen as a goddess figure is in clear contrast to the uniform denunciation of her in his early plays. This progression of Helen's characterization in Euripides' plays, together with the scattered references to her as fertility "goddess" in Greek culture over four hundred years, culminates in a striking possibility of meaning for us — something which surpasses the *Oxford Classical Dictionary*'s citation of Helen as "one of the most plausible examples of a 'faded goddess'."[16]

The waning and waxing attached to the meaning of "Helen" combines in one figure the dichotomies of figures of women in androcentric cultures noticed by other feminist critics. Toril Moi, for example, explicating Kristeva's notion of the marginality of women with respect to the symbolic order, thinks that

> women seen as the limit of the symbolic order
> will ... share in the disconcerting properties of
> *all* frontiers: they will be neither inside nor
> outside, neither known nor unknown. It is this
> position that has enabled male culture sometimes
> to vilify women as representing darkness and

chaos, to view them as Lilith or the Whore of
Babylon, and sometimes to elevate them as the
representatives of a higher and purer nature, to
venerate them as Virgins and Mothers of
God.[17]

The figure of Helen as both vilified and venerated represents an
especially rich case study of marginality and can be illuminated
by means of Moi's general comment on marginality: "In the
first instance the borderline is seen as part of the chaotic
wilderness outside, and in the second it is seen as an inherent
part of the inside: the part that protects and shields the symbolic
order from the imaginary chaos" (ibid.). In Version One of the
myth, Helen's beauty remains a seductive power and a bounty
to be won. At the same time, by blaming her for the war's
tragedies, Greece did not have to face its own ambiguous
motives for waging the war.

But by moving to Version Two of the myth in the later
plays, Euripides also represents Helen in terms of what Kristeva
calls a new ethic, one based not on "Spinoza's biologically-
based exclusion of women from ethical decision-making," but
instead in a process which expects and involves otherness,
distance, and limitation. Indeed, Euripides' plays can be
viewed as making possible what Kristeva calls "a structure, a
logical discourse ... that takes two stages into account, the
conscious and the unconscious ones, and two corresponding
types of performances."[18] As we have seen, the fact that
Version Two is developed over and against Version One can be
read as a struggle between two kinds of ethics in which
benevolence overcomes vengeance. Clearly the play *Helen* is
a full-blown dramatization of Helen as actively restoring
Menelaus and his companions to their homeland and overcoming
their mistrust in order to be able to do so. In *Orestes*, Apollo
rescues the Helen of Version One from murder by Orestes and

Pylades, after which she takes on the divine status of Version Two. In another dramatic instance of a mortal achieving divine status in Euripides' plays, Thetis, at the end of *Andromache*, comes to make Peleus, her husband, a divinity forever after he has just suffered the loss of his two sons. In all these instances, the elevation of a human to god/ess might be said to be based on an ethic of love, i.e., a love expressing itself as penultimate justice.

As goddess, Helen also participates in an interesting shift in the concept of power in Euripides. One can see a parallel between *Helen* and *The Bacchae* in the sense that both Helen and Dionysus represent, in their respective plays, new conceptions of the divine. Dionysus understands himself as a god, even though the people of Thebes are divided on the issue of his identity. Helen understands herself as a person acted upon by the gods, even though the Chorus refers to her both as the daughter of Zeus and the daughter of Tyndareus. But where divinity is "most terrible, yet most gentle to mankind" in *The Bacchae* (ll. 860), so, too, in *Helen* the gods are "complex ... hard for us to predict" (ll. 712). In both plays, the notion of deity is ambiguous and intrinsically linked with human action. Helen is spoken of as having never "shamed her aged father ... [or her] divine brothers..." (11. 720-21) and in this play is given the favor of the gods. Dionysus is said to have come to Thebes in *The Bacchae* to exact retribution for the slander of his mother's character because she conceived a child by Zeus. Dionysus breaks the sheer force of Pentheus' brute physical power and arrogance and lets loose the force of madness. Helen becomes a guide and savior to the Greeks, even though she professes ignorance of what to do next herself and seemingly chances upon successful courses of action. Helen, too, is the site of a remarkable lament in *Helen* which includes all those oppressed (both Trojans and Greeks) by the Trojan War: the daughters of Troy, Priam's people, Achaeans killed in the war, their wives, Achaeans drowned. The myths of Helen fortuitously complicate the God/power issue so easily reduced to heteronomy in classical discussions of the gods and goddesses.

These images of godliness are different from the essentialist notion of God, which Kristeva describes as meaning which has been bestowed on an "Other (the absolute signifier, God)."[19] Neither polytheism nor monotheism seems adequate to conceptualize Euripides' treatment of the gods. Perhaps some new concept is needed — one which signifies both the unity of existence and the many ways this unity is represented. And on the issue of destiny, it seems clear that as one response to this question, the figure of Helen represents the multifaceted phenomena which are gathered together in this concept: on the one hand, the experience of being acted on, being chosen, being graced and empowered; and on the other, the experience of seizing the moment, playing things by ear, getting a life, taking decisive action.

Is it possible to claim some mitigating effects of Euripidean texts upon the androcentric world? We have seen that Helen herself as the emergence of a new goddess at the end of Euripides' work in some sense is like Dionysus as the emergence of a new god in *The Bacchae* (no longer singly executed interventionist power). We might see in these dramatic actions the strength in the power of the "affect" that Kristeva posits — that welling up of resistance to the reified symbolic order. Kristeva cautions, on the one hand, against the temptation to ignore social/political structures by emphasizing the "affective," and on the other, against the temptation to ignore the complex process by which sex differences get positioned into the symbolic order. And while Helen and Dionysus are dissimilar in several ways, they both represent in different ways the freedom of god/ess to be god/ess and to be so as the space and ground of new possibilities.

Applied to goddess research, Kristeva's caution can also assist us in constructing a critical typology for a religious understanding of goddess figures. In the first generation of research, goddess traditions are retrieved for the purpose of maintaining equality between female and male models for human aspirations and behavior. In the second generation of research, aspects traditionally regarded as feminine (and therefore of less or negative value than those traditionally regarded as masculine) are transvaluated to gain new worth. Thus far, goddess research has been primarily of the first and second types. What is needed in the third generation of goddess research is a study of the historical fluctuations of god and goddess figures in relation to the possibilities for human existence at any given time and place.

What can be said specifically of fertility goddesses in this three-fold typology? In the first two stages, fertility goddesses are too often celebrated only for their ties to nature and new life. Only in the third generation are the limitations of the fertility figure made explicit: first, it is recognized that fertility figure goddesses are not the only deities that have links to nature. Second, it is discovered that fertility imagery is entangled with other imagery and may even have obscured it.[20] In the case of Helen, however, the reverse seems to be the case: namely, that other imagery has obscured the fertility imagery. When other imagery comes to the fore, two effects occur first, the obscuration and eventual loss of fertility imagery and the fading of divine status, and second, the opposition to fertility imagery by historic religion which sought to free human beings from their dependency on natural forces. The transformation of Helen from a fertility goddess to a marginal figure of beauty and blame thus lends itself to investigation as a third generation goddess research problem.

III.   Yeats' Poem, "No Second Troy": Appropriating the Tradition

But who is Helen for us, we moderns with prodigious memories? Yeats' poem, "No Second Troy," is one modern appropriation of Helen.

No Second Troy (1910)

Why should I blame her that she filled my days
With misery, or that she would of late
Have taught to ignorant men most violent ways,
Or hurled the little streets upon the great,
Had they but courage equal to desire?
What could have made *her* peaceful with a mind
That nobleness made simple as a fire,
With beauty like a tightened bow, a kind
That is not natural in an age like this,
Being high and solitary and most stern?
Why, what could she have done, being what she is?
Was there another Troy for her to burn?[21]

If we ask with Yeats, "Who is Helen for us?" we find ourselves cannily inscribed in a dialectic of reader and historical image through the rhetorical question, "Was there another Troy for her to burn?" There is no escaping the task of self definition as well as re-definition of the received tradition — a task that poetry and myth, perhaps especially that which makes reference to public figures, imposes.

What interests us especially is that the poem's portrayal of "what she is" reiterates the themes of blame and praise. In this sense, the poem is characteristic of the contemporary memory of Helen. But unlike popular memory which would either praise or blame Helen, Yeats does not dichotomize the

two themes. The persona of the poem will not blame her:
"Why, what could she have done,/ being what she is?" Nor is
the persona superficial about what constitutes beauty: "... with
a mind/ that nobleness made simple as a fire, with beauty like
a tightened bow...." As a result, Yeats' Helen is complex and
multi-dimensional. The genius of the last line is that it metony-
mizes the "her" who set fire to Troy with Helen — without ever
naming Helen, so vivid is that part of her memory for us. Nor
does the self-referent have to be stated: The poet is Troy and it
is he who has been set aflame.

Yeats' answer, then, is to ask a question: what could
Helen have done? Whether we read the poem as pertaining to
Maude Gonne or to Helen, Yeats' answer is that there was no
other Troy for her than the one which became her entrance into
history, memory, and the poem. That she burned Troy is the
vital truth to Yeats' conception of who she is.

Can Helen be otherwise? We have reasons to expect so.
But those other figures affirmed as true will not be any less
complex than the ones reflected on here.

Notes

1. Reformist feminist theologians, such as Rosemary Ruether
    and Elizabeth Schüssler Fiorenza, in different ways, have
    brought criticism to bear on goddess religions. Radical
    feminist theologians, such as Mary Daly, often see
    goddess religions as substituting a female dominance for
    one that is male. But see also the constructive theology
    of Carol Christ.

2. See Deborah Cameron, *Feminism and Linguistic Theory*
    (New York: Macmillan, 1985).

3. Cf. Carol Christ's "Symbols of Goddess and God in Feminist Theology," in Carl Olson, *The Book of the Goddess Past and Present* (New York: Crossroad, 1983), pp. 231-50, and unpublished lectures on God and contemporary thought by David Tracy at the University of Chicago, 1988-89.

4. Aphrodite, Hera, and Athena all claimed possession of the apple of discord. Paris was chosen to settle the dispute: Hera offered him riches and royal greatness; Athena, success in war; and Aphrodite, the most beautiful woman.

5. C.M. Bowra, "Stesichorus" in *The Oxford Classical Dictionary*, Second Edition, ed. by N.G.L. Hammond and H.H. Scullard (Oxford: Clarendon Press, 1970), p. 1012-13.

6. The two forms of the variant Egypt story were as follows: first, as in Herodotus, Paris Alexander was blown off course to Egypt on his way back from Greece to Troy with Helen, and Proteus thwarted Paris' kidnapping of Helen by sending Paris off without Helen; second, as in the version used by Euripides, Apollo rescues Helen and transports her to Egypt.

7. Besides Pausanius 3.19.10, 8.23.6-7, and Theocritus 18.43ff., see Martin P. Nilsson, *Geschichte der Griechischen Religion*, I (1955), p. 475. M.L. West's Helen (*Immortal Helen*, 1975) by contrast is a one-dimensional figure: "To poets throughout the ages she has served as the paragon of beauty. Her delinquency is forgiven." Walter Burkert affirmed her divine lineage: "... in Sparta Helen was clearly a goddess" (Burkert, *Greek Religion*, 1985, p. 205). The *Oxford Classical Dictionary*, 2nd ed., surmised that "[H]er non-Greek name, her association

with trees ... and her connexion with birds ... all fit an ancient, pre-Hellenic goddess, probably connected with vegetation and fertility, better than a dimly remembered princess, or even a purely imaginary human member of an ancient royal family. It is in no wise impossible that an old deity traditionally worshipped by the pre-Dorian population of Laconia had been taken, long before Homer, for an ancestress of their kings." Helen is also referred to as a daemon (see Burkert, pp. 179-81). In *The Religion of Greece in Prehistoric Times* (Berkeley: University of California Press, 1942), Alex Persson did not hesitate to group Helen, along with Pasiphaë, Europa, Diktynna, Eileithyia, Aridela, and Aphaia, as "invocations of the same deity" (p. 135). For an elaboration of Helen's association with the Minoan tree cult, see also Martin P. Nilsson, *The Minoan-Mycenaean Religion and Its Survival in Greek Religion* (Lund: C.W.K. Gleerup, 1950), esp. pp. 551-52.

8. Hesiod and Homer both state that Helen was the daughter of Zeus and that her beauty surpassed the beauty of all mortal women, thus implying some generic distinction between mortals and Helen. I am indebted to Paula Sage for calling my attention to the parallel between Helen and Demeter.   See also Froma I. Zeitlin, "Travesties of gender and genre in Aristophanes' *Thesmophoriazousae*," in Helen Foley, ed., *Reflections of Women in Antiquity* (London and Paris: Gordon and Breach, 1982), esp. pp. 186ff, 197ff.

9. The David Grene and Richmond Lattimore editions of the plays (Chicago: The University of Chicago Press, 1955-59) have been used throughout.

10. In her *Chronology of the Extant Plays of Euripides*, Grace Harriet Macurdy (New York: Haskell House, 1966) describes the criteria used in determining the dates of the ten plays which are not dated by ancient testimony.

11. Kristeva's explicit attitudes toward religion vary. Whenever she speaks of religion as an ideology, she would have religion *replaced by* aesthetic discourse. In *Tales of Love* (1987), she is better reader of particular figures (Bernard) than when she attempts to describe religion in general, e.g., Christianity (really, Paul). On the whole, her treatment of religion parallels her treatment of literary theory, which is both deconstructive and constructively analytic. In her early work, she considers the terms "faith" and "religious" essentialist categories, opposed to feminine discourse which is individuating, flowing, political. In her later investigations, e.g., "Stabat Mater," she emphasized the ambiguity of religious figures with respect to psychoanalytic meaning.

    I am aware that some of Kristeva's readers criticize her work for not being feminist and, more recently, for not being sufficiently political. Toril Moi has answered these criticisms in *Sexual/Textual Politics* (London: Methuen, 1987). See especially pp. 150-173, where Moi argues that Kristeva's contributions to feminist theory far outweigh the shortcomings of her work. For another insightful explication of Kristeva's thought, see Elizabeth Gross, "Philosophy, subjectivity and the body" in *Feminist Challenges: Social and Political Theory*, ed. by Carole Pateman and Elizabeth Gross (Boston: Northeastern University Press, 1986), 125-26, 152.

12. See Book I of Herodotus, *Persian History*. Herodotus outlined a "domino effect" of causes for the Trojan War.

According to the wise men of Persia, the Phoenicians
were the first offenders: when the women of Argos,
including Io, the king's daughter, came down to the
Phoenician ship and bought merchandise, the Phoenicians
"cried one to another and rushed upon them. Then most
of the women escaped, but Io with others was ravished;
and they put them in the ship, and departed and sailed
away unto Egypt." Next some Greeks sailed to Tyre in
Phoenicia and ravished the king's daughter, Europa.
"Thus far, it was like for like, but thereafter the Greeks
were the cause of the second wrong: they ravished the
king's daughter, Medea, at Aea of the Colchians. By
means of an ambassador, the king of the Colchians
demanded satisfaction and the restoration of his daughter.
But the Greeks replied that the Colchians had not given
them satisfaction for the ravishment of Io, so they would-
n't give satisfaction for Medea." In the next generation,
Alexander, son of Priam and Hecuba, "having heard these
things, conceived the desire to get a wife from Greece by
ravishing her, knowing surely that he should not need to
give satisfaction, because they also give none. So he
ravished Helen...." The Greeks demanded restoration and
satisfaction, were refused. "Now thus far they did but
ravish women one from another. But thereafter they say
that the Greeks were greatly at fault, for the Greeks began
to make war on Asia before they made war on Europe.
The Persians hold that to ravish women is wicked, but to
be eager for revenge after they are ravished they hold is
foolish."

Some feminist classicists see in this history a
founding of male civilization on the raped bodies of
women. For another theory which accounts for male
dominance in archetypal situations like the one described
in Herodotus, a theory which is compatible with Kristeva's psychoanalytical approach, see Eli Sagan, *At the*

Dawn of Tyranny: The Origins of Individualism, Political Oppression, and the State (New York: Alfred A. Knopf, 1985). See also an application of Sagan's theory in Katherine K. Young, "Introduction," in *Women in World Religions*, ed. by Arvind Sharma (Albany: SUNY Press, 1987).

13. A good example of this positivist kind of reading can be found in A.W. Verrall's *Euripides the Rationalist* (1905).

14. Julia Kristeva, "Talking about *Polylogue*," in Toril Moi, ed., *French Feminist Thought: A Reader* (London: Basil Blackwell, 1987), p. 110.

15. Kristeva, *Tales of Love* (New York: Columbia University Press, 1987), p. 169.

16. The *Oxford Classical Dictionary* refers to Helen as a 'faded goddess' without alluding to her restoration, except to observe that "the mere fact of being her husband is Menelaus' passport to Elysium" (*Od.* 4. 569).

17. Toril Moi, *Sexual/Textual Politics* (London: Metheun, 1987), p. 167.

18. Kristeva, *Desire in Language* (New York: Columbia University Press, 1980), p. ix.

19. Kristeva, "Talking about *Polylogue*," p. 111.

20. See the remarkable essay by Marymay Downing, "Prehistoric Goddesses: The Cretan Challenge," *Journal of Feminist Studies in Religion*, 1 (Spring, 1985), 7-22, which shows how the seafaring and technological imagery of Minoan goddesses has been obscured by fertility

imagery. Downing also cautions that "faith in a goddess ... may have been conceived among the ancient Cretans in quite simple terms, or in thealogically complex and profound terms, and the full range in between as well, just as religious beliefs vary among individuals, and over an individual's lifetime" (14).

21. William Butler Yeats, "No Second Troy," in *The Poems: A New Edition*, ed. by Richard J. Finneran (New York: Macmillan, 1983), p. 91.

THREE FACES OF THE GREAT GODDESS: SHULAMITE, CINDERELLA, BLACK VIRGIN

Denyse Rockey

"I am black but beautiful"[1]

    This assertion by the Shulamite provides support for Bayley's contention that *The Song of Songs* "is not only a bridge linking theology to folk-lore, but it contains several finger-posts pointing definitely to the story known nowadays as *Cinderella*."[2] Further, he suggests, the heroine's extraordinary robe changes furnish "not only the clue to the allegoric significance of *Cinderella* herself," but they also throw "unexpected light" upon *The Song of Songs*.[3] These changes tell of her fluctuating fortunes from forbearing ash-sitter, shepherdess or goosegirl to radiant princess. Since the lowly Cinderella is frequently described as black, it should be elucidating to explore any affinity she might have with the Shulamite, to whom shame[4], scorching and menial work were not unfamiliar. "Look not upon me," she pleads, "because I am black"[5] — this is but a legacy of being sent to toil in her brothers' vineyards.[6] Thus the Shulamite, a rustic lass, contrasts with the sophisticated Daughters of Jerusalem, who act as chorus in *The Song*. Inferior class, however, is no barrier to her being linked with Solomon, who himself might rank as a CinderLad in one Talmudic legend. This tells how, following Asmodeus' theft of his magic ring, Solomon eventually became lover of an Ammonite princess whose father, the king, he was obliged to serve as scullion.[7]

The Shulamite's assertion also articulates the spirit of an ancient, femininely toned, religious movement that had no clear beginning[8] but offered fertile soil for the rise in Europe, during the Crusades,[9] of the Cult of the Black Virgin,[10] for which it provided a recurrent theme.[11] Of such importance were her words that she, Bride of *The Song of Songs*, became likened to Mary, Mother of the Church[12] and herself the Bride of Christ. So close was their association that in Santa Maria de Trastevere, Mary is depicted as the Shulamite in a mosaic possibly inspired by St. Bernard of Clairvaux, the great 12th century commentator on *The Song of Songs*, during a visit to Rome.[13] In Paris, another church displays a mural of the Blessed Virgin beneath an angel, who holds a scroll on which is written in Latin: "I am black but beautiful."[14]

Notwithstanding lack of enthusiasm for Black Virgin statues by many of their modern clerical custodians,[15] the Catholic Church has shown no reticence in comparing Mary to the Shulamite on grounds other than complexion. These, amongst other likenesses, also provide points of comparison with Cinderella.

First, in a hymn Mary is spoken of as Abishag,[16] who was David's nurse in his declining days.[17] The most beautiful girl in all Israel, she came from Shunem[18] on which account 'Shunemite' has come to be synonymous with 'a beauty'[19] and consequently could well apply to the glittering Cinderella. As Eusebius equated the town of Shunem with Shulem, one tradition has identified the Shulamite of *The Song of Songs*[20] with Abishag[21] and hence she with the Virgin.

Metaphors provide a second point of comparison, again through the Shulamite's words:[22]

I am the rose of Sharon,
And the lily of the valleys.

What these flowers actually were matters little; how they have
been conceived in Western consciousness is important and may
be summarised:

> The lily and the rose combine,
> The wisdom and the love divine.

Whoever the true author, it is symbolically fitting that *The Song
of Songs* be attributed to Solomon,[23] that great lover of women
and embodiment of wisdom.   Later we shall discuss the
connection our women have with wisdom.   Here it is the heart
that is in question.   Solomon's poem is pre-eminently a love-
song on which the highest human affections might be modelled;
representing completion, perfection and consummate achievement,[24] the rose belongs to it.   According to Christian tradition, the rose grew in Paradise without thorns; consequently,
Mary, the Unfallen, is associated with this flower.   The Rosary
is hers.[25]   As the 'wheel of being,' the rose is connected with
Mary, the sea or womb from which Christ and his Church were
born.   The movement is from earth to heaven.   When thorny
and red, the rose represents spiritual blossoming through
struggle and sacrifice.[26]   Thus a hymn praises Christ as the
Rose of Sharon.   The Shulamite neglected herself in serving her
brothers.[27]   And as Cinderella was a model of self-sacrifice it
is not surprising to find the rose featuring in versions of her
story.   It may name the heroine,[28] entitle the story[29] or carry
the plot forward.[30]   The Shulamite amidst the Daughters of
Jerusalem is further likened to "a lily amongst thorns": [31] yet
another description of the Virgin.[32]   Cinderella amidst her
carping step-relatives would similarly fit the analogy; one
heroine was actually thrown into a briar bush by the malefac-
tors.[33]   The lily is of the valley, indicating humiliation and
travail;[34] and blossoming early, it marks Advent.[35]   Contrary
to the rose, it represents love descending from heaven.   Its
worth exceeds even Solomon's glory.[36]   Delicate and pale, the

lily essentially symbolises chastity, purity and Mary Immaculate.[37] This leads to a fourth point. So superlative is the Shulamite's beauty that she is without blemish[38]: the original stainless and perpetual condition of the Virgin Mary, full of grace and hence qualified for divine motherhood according to Catholic dogma.

Several theories are forwarded regarding the proper interpretation of *The Song of Songs*,[39] but given its highly sensual tone Jews and Christians alike have found it difficult to resolve with their religious scruples or psychological inhibitions. Before the 18th century most tended to see it as an allegory of the love of Yahweh for Israel or Christ for his Church. Yet how could the metaphor stand if the human relationship on which it draws is lewd, sinful and inimical to literal interpretation? Love with its unions and separations entails heartbeats and tears, whoever the object. As Raymond Lull, that holy 13th century Christian troubadour and mystic, wrote in *The Book of the Lover and the Beloved* (v. 82):

> They asked the Beloved about the love of his Lover. He answered, 'It is a mingling of joy and sorrow, fervour and fear'.

Nor is the body forgotten by Mother Julian of Norwich:[40]

> In the self-same point where the soul is made sensual, in the self-same point is the city of God ordained from without beginning.

Emotional transports and yearnings are concrete experiences best expressed in physical terms. Such experiences engage the whole person. The other-directed will and intellect are clothed in sensations, feelings and images which they elevate without becoming divorced from them, as is most evident in St. John of the Cross' *Spiritual Canticle*, which reflects much of Solomon's *Song*.

Since the Shulamite's virginity *per se* is not at issue, her flawlessness is taken to signify chastity. Both exemplary states rest upon integrity. As if fearing the serpent might again rear its head, the Church has often presented a rather sanitised image of the second Eve. A separation then becomes discernible between the pale, abstract model of maternal purity and the warm intimacy normally associated with nurture. Thus the commendable feminine principle in Christianity is threatened by being ungrounded; that is, severed from its physical and historical roots. The Virgin may have more intellectual rationale than emotional appeal for those who first meet her through genteel statues and pious phrases. With the picture of an obedient servant or dutiful wife frequently predominating, it is small wonder that Robert Graves should see in the impassive and predictable Mary the qualities and limitations of patriarchal society's ideal woman. She is the veiled, vestal virgin, presiding deity of the hearth and guardian spirit of humans, who was deified by the Latins as Vesta and the Greeks as Hestia.[41] In this goddess also lies the sorrowful, toiling Cinderella who leaves for the ball entreating:[42]

> Little angels, guardian angels,
> protect the house whilst I'm away.

Never forgetting her duties, this melancholy maiden might be seen as an exemplar of several beatitudes. The risks she takes to evade the unnatural advances of her father certainly speak of her chastity.[43]

Despite his distaste for domesticity, Graves does concede that the Blessed Virgin has inspired princes, poets, saints and soldiers.[44] And notwithstanding her conscientiousness, Cinderella did ignite the heart of her lover and become a princess. Why is this so? Because of an invisible spark, Bayley suggests.

Cinderella is the shining one "who sits among the cinders and keeps the fire alight," she "is a personification of the Holy Spirit dwelling unhonoured amid the smouldering ashes of the Soul's latent, never totally extinct Divinity." She, by patient tending, fans them into flames. Through the Finnish Cinderella, Tuna, a diminutive of Kristuna or Christina, he sees "Christ personified as a little girl."[45] The brilliance of Cinderella, the fire-tender, lies hidden beneath soot; the brilliance of the Shulamite, exposed to the sun's rays, lies hidden beneath a weather-beaten skin. The brilliance of the Virgin, whose special feast is Candlemas, may lie hidden beneath dark lacquer, though some say she became soiled by smoke from flames of surrounding votive candles.[46] This often ignored Black Lady is the Virgin's other aspect and, perhaps, it is she who has greater claim to guardianship of the sacred fire.

Fifthly, these women are élite representatives of their sex and therefore specially chosen. Although a drudge, a Chinese Cinderella is "as beautiful as a goddess" and pursued by the king.[47] Although a tender of vines, the Shulamite is sought by her Bridegroom because she is "most beautiful among women,"[48] superior to a harem of sixty queens, eighty concubines and numerous maidens;[49] she alone is a dove, perfect, unique.[50] Although a lowly maidservant of the Lord,[51] to be delivered in a stable,[52] Mary is highly favoured and thus blessed among women.[53] Considering this exaltation of the servant,[54] the revelation of Cinderella's uniqueness while she is black, ragged and relegated to the hearth takes on greater meaning. From all the fine ladies of the land, the prince is able to choose Cinderella because of her petite foot, an endowment implying refinement.[55] Consequently, Bayley takes the Bridegroom's praise:[56]

> How beautiful are your feet in sandals,
> O prince's daughter!

as a further text linking folk-lore and theology. Indeed, this sixth of our comparisons he sees as the principal point of contact between the fairy-tale and *The Song of Songs*.[57]

Feet bespeak moving forwards and this action is clearer in the alternative translation 'footsteps.' St. John of the Cross sees the royal inheritance of the holy soul, Bride of his *Canticle* yearning for her Spouse, expressed in the above verse from *The Song*.[58] Progress towards regal status involves many Cinderellas in redemption, in reclaiming their lost station, which itself implies a fall.[59] Though immaculate from conception, the humble Mary grew in virtue and is now celebrated as Queen by the faithful. The Shulamite's path is less certain but, whatever her social rank, in uniting with the archetypal Solomon she was elevated to Queen of Wisdom. The historical Solomon is known to have married a Pharoah's daughter. The meaning of 'Egyptian' is a 'black';[60] the meaning of 'Ethiopian' is 'Burnt-face.'[61] This would account for Ronald Knox's depiction of the Shulamite's complexion as 'Ethiop.' Perhaps she was only a simple vine-tender. Perhaps she had rank but approached Solomon in humility. There actually is one such contender for the title of Bride: Sheba, Queen of Ethiopia, who sincerely sought instruction from the wisest of men. *The Song of Songs* has been seen as their epithalamion.[62]

Parallels can now be drawn perhaps between Abraham and Hagar,[63] certainly between Moses and his Ethiopian wife,[64] Solomon and the Shulamite, Christ and the Black Virgin, to which list it would not be frivolous to add Prince Charming and Cinderella.

The sun that scorches, Origen notes, is the selfsame sun that illuminates.[65] The Shulamite does not remain dark or melancholy for at the end of the paean we read:[66]

Who is this that cometh up,
having been made white,
and leaning on her Nephew?

Knox renders this verse:[67]

> Who is this that maketh her way
> up the desert road, *all gaily clad*,
> leaning on the arm of her true love?

Whilst most translators omit the words I have italicised, we know that some remarkable transformation has taken place because earlier the Beloved asks:[68]

> Who is this arising like the dawn,
> fair as the moon,
> resplendent as the sun ...?

The answer could well be: Cinderella in her ballgowns, one like the dawn, one like the moon and a third like the sun.[69] Many other metaphors are used to convey her radiance. Often a star glistens from her forehead[70] and one heroine is as lovely as her mother who has "stars round her brow, a sun on the top, and a moon at the back, of her head."[71] Sometimes Cinderella is helped by a 'beautiful kind lady.' Literally a god-mother, she is none other than the Holy Virgin herself.[72] The Virgin Mary's resplendence mirrors the Sun of Justice.[73] In St. Andrew's missal Schemata for her Assumption, reflection is recommended on the Old Testament passage:[74]

> The princess is decked in her chamber
> with gold-woven robes;
> in many-coloured robes is she led to the king.

and the New Testament text:[75]

> A great portent appeared in heaven,
> a woman clothed with the sun,

with the moon under her feet,
and on her head a crown of twelve stars.

This woman of the Apocalypse is explicitly identified by Pius X as the Blessed Virgin.[76] St. Bernard elucidates the celestial symbolism: "every holy soul is itself ... a heaven with Understanding for its sun, Faith for its moon, and Virtues for its stars."[77]

An eighth comparison centers on the event which *The Song of Songs* celebrates: the wedding of the Lover and the Beloved. The potential fruitfulness of their union is glimpsed in the banqueting hall. Overcome by the moment, the Bride calls for sustenance:[78]

Stay me with flagons,
comfort me with apples

which has been phrased:[79]

Feed me with raisin cakes,
restore me with apples.

Other versions picture her cushioned on flowers and revived by apricots. Such delights, characteristic of the whole poem, bring to mind the wonder experienced by Basile's Cat Cinderella when first setting eyes upon the feast:[80]

Where did all the tarts and cakes come from?
Where all the stews and rissoles,
all the macaroni and graviuoli?

A gloss reveals 'stews' to be comprised of: a good piece of tender meat, garlic, pine-seeds, raisins, sugar, almonds and cinnamon.[81] Cornucopia is a significant motif in the Cinderella Cycle.[82] A ball is not the only venue for feasting. Some

Cinderellas encounter the prince at a wedding, which prefigures their own marriage. We have no record of rejoicing by the Virgin when united with the Holy Spirit, her Spouse, only of her consternation during the Visitation.[83] Perhaps festivities were delayed until the wedding in Cana of Galilee where, concerned by the empty liquor jars, Mary occasioned Jesus' first miracle — the turning of water into superlative wine,[84] signalling the intoxication in store for those baptised in a greater spirit. We may presume that the Blessed Virgin is now enjoying the Eschatological Banquet.

A further similarity between the Biblical song and the folk-tale Bayley finds in the parlous condition of the Bride,[85] whom he equates with the Maiden in *The Wedding Song of Wisdom*, a poem in the Apocryphal *Acts of St. Thomas*, on account of a door-opening sequence.[86] For the Shulamite, this symbol features in a dream. On hearing knocking, she opens the door to her Bridegroom, only to find he has departed. Desperate to seek him out, she walks the streets and suffers the abuse meted out to women of the night.[87] Distraught, she seeks help:[88]

> I charge you, O Daughters of Jerusalem,
> If you find my Beloved,
> That you tell him I am love sick.

At a later time, it is the Bridegroom who is anguished, and he appeals:[89]

> Return, return, O Shulamite;
> Return, return, that we may look upon you.

These could be the words of the love-sick prince after Cinderella had fled the ball. His plight is best conveyed in Catskin versions of the Cycle where he languishes in bed, unable to eat.[90] Obliged to return to the ashes, we can imagine how

Cinderella herself felt. Most tales tell of her capacity to weep.
Tears were also familiar to the Virgin, Our Lady of Sorrows;
sometimes they were shed by her statues.[91] At the foot of the
Cross, her grief reached its nadir and amongst the early
Christians, her anticipation of the Second Coming must have
been the greatest. But what is this longing? Who is the Bride?
Bayley endorses St. Bernard's view that she is none other than
"the soul thirsting for God."[92]

Lastly, Bayley finds a correspondence between the
Bridegroom's words:[93]

> You have ravished my heart,
> my sister, my spouse

and a tale in the Cinderella Cycle entitled: *The Brother and
Sister*,[94] where the brother does duty for the prince. Two
orphans are heirs to a rich kingdom and the sister's beauty
induces the young man to seek her hand in marriage. In one of
the few instances of an unhappy ending, the heroine is swal-
lowed into the ground as, bedecked in her wedding dress, she
cries:[95]

> Open earth! open wide!
> For to be a brother's bride,
> Is an awful sin.

In another highly unusual tale, the heroine appears to succumb
to her brother's ardour though the eventual outcome is uncertain
as "they leave the house together, but none knows whither they
go." Surprisingly, this is the same girl who had resisted the
advances of her own father and a ferryman.[96] An unnatural
father is a principal motif in stories of the Catskin type.[97] The
plot turns on a heroine who, having extracted magnificent
dresses from her hopeful father, runs away disguised in an
animal's fell, takes service in a palace and bewitches the prince

when she appears in full splendour at the ball. Incest has also
been seen in Cap O'Rushes tales where the heroine is banished
by a Lear-type father.[98]   However, there are hints that her
chastity may not be as total as these stories imply.   The
sobriquet Hearth Cat has sexual connotations that cannot be
elaborated here.[99]   Little need be said about the Virgin Mary,
whose 'relationships' with her Father, Spouse and Son are as
mysterious as the Trinity Itself.

From the foregoing discussion it is not difficult to see
why Cinderella and the Shulamite have been characterised as
"protean, elusive and contradictory."[100]   Well could they
speak the words of Afterthought, the Gnostic manifestation of
Wisdom and female instructing principle, uttered in *The
Thunder, Perfect Intellect*:[101]

> For, it is I who am the first: and the last.
> It is I who am the revered: and the despised.
> It is I who am the harlot: and the holy.
> It is I who am the wife: and the virgin.
> It is I who am the mother: and the daughter.
> I am the members of my mother.
> It is I who am barren: and who has many children.
> It is I who am the one whose marriage is magnificent:
>   and who have not married.
> It is I who am the midwife: and she who does not give
>   birth.
> It is I who am consolation: of my own travail.
> It is I who am the bride: and the bridegroom.

Varying though their manifestations may be, the recurring
themes in the foregoing comparative study are: blackness,
brilliance, grief, maternity, fire-tending, lowliness, queenship,
uniqueness, beauty, sensuality, purity and incest.   Their
connection can hardly be accidental but their point of unity is as
elusive as the women in question.

Despite extensive scholarship, the origin, authorship and interpretation of *The Song of Songs* continues to puzzle, while the Shulamite herself remains inaccessible to logical analysts. In no way have they tarnished her image or diminished her perpetual fascination — and herein lies a clue. Fascination is the hallmark of unconscious energetic activity, the compelling character of which is the dynamic component of an archetypal psychic structure, having biophysical effects and determining behaviour, that is unknowable in itself. As its essence, content or inherent meaning may only be grasped by those having highly developed awareness, and then only with much effort, it is generally manifested to consciousness through figurative speech, myth and symbols, the polyvalent nature of which depends upon the degree of the archetype's fragmentation; i.e., its polarities have crystallised out into several opposing images.[102]

Are, then, Cinderella, the Shulamite and the Virgin representatives of an archetype and, if so, which? Is there an axis around which its contradictory aspects revolve, waxing and waning like the moon, alternating like the seasons? Fertility and its twin, creativity, are the clear answer. Birth and re-birth imply decay, but they are not necessarily antithetical if decay is considered a necessary prerequisite for renewal. "If we accept this paradox," Woodman sagely points out, "we are not torn to pieces by what seems to be an intolerable contradiction. Birth is the death of life we have known: death is the birth of the life we have yet to live. We need to hold the tensions and allow our circuit to give way to a larger circumference."[103] This greater round is the object of our search: the Great Mother.[104] A supreme example is Isis.

Isis was a principle female deity whose cult flourished between 1700-1100 B.C., the period preceding the earliest date proposed for *The Song of Songs*.[105] Of significance is the fact the she was Egyptian and frequently portrayed as black.[106] By now, some of her titles will have a familiar

ring: Queen Isis, Royal Wife and Sister, Lady of Heaven, Great
Mother, Mother of the Gods, Opener of the Ways, Star of the
Sea.[107]   In the Temple at Luxor where Isis animates figures
of the body and soul, she says: "I inflame the hearts of hundreds and thousands."[108]   Flowers associated with her are the
rose, lotus and water-lily.[109]   One of her representations is as
a queen standing on a crescent moon and surrounded by twelve
stars.[110]

  The crescent moon mirrors two horns and hence the
great cow-goddess, Hathor, with whom Isis was often equated.
Her mother was said to be the celestial cow, Nut, depicted in
human form as a dark skinned woman covered with stars
bending over the earth god.[111]   In Hathor's udder lies the
nourishing aspect of Isis who is sometimes depicted suckling a
pharaoh or her son, Horus. The pair provided a model for later
images of the Madonna and Child.[112]   Black Virgin statues
are said to produce milk,[113] three drops of which nourished
the three-year-old Bernard of Clairvaux.[114]   Significantly, it
is from India, land of the Sacred Cow and possible source of
The Song of Songs,[115] that an analogous Cinderella story
comes. After a complicated sequence of events in which the
heroine marries the prince and produces two babies that her
scheming sisters think they have killed at birth, she is reunited
with them some years later when they appear at the palace and,
as confirmation of their identity, demand that seven curtains be
placed between them and their mother. Immediately: "Three
streams of milk burst from her breasts, and, penetrating the
seven curtains, run into the children's mouths."[116]   In European versions of the story, the cow features prominently in the
fairy-godmother role. Thus, she may be equated with the
Hathors, the cow-goddess multiplied by seven, who were god-
mothers to young children.[117]   The cow feeds the starving
Cinderella or completes an impossible spinning task. Once
discovered, the step-mother has the animal killed but the cow's
benevolence continues through a magic tree that springs from

her grave and dispenses fine clothes at the appropriate moment.[118]   Greater meaning now accrues to the voluptuousness of the Shulamite.[119]

Opinions vary considerably regarding the etymology of 'Isis.'   It is said to mean 'throne,' or, combined with Maat, 'ancient wisdom.'[120]   According to Plutarch, it comes from 'Ursa,' denoting 'knowledge.'[121]   Bayley argues that 'is' and 'ish' originally signified 'light.'[122]   If this be so, then Is-is would match the radiance of Cinderella, Shulamite and Virgin. Graves, however, states:[123]

> Isis is an onomatopoeic Asianic word, Ish-Ish,
> meaning 'she who weeps,' because the moon was
> held to scatter dew and because Isis, the pre-
> Christian original of the *Mater Dolorosa*,
> mourned for Osiris when Set killed him.

Isis' complex family relationships also match those of our three women. She was the sister-wife of Osiris and virgin-mother of Horus, conceived after his father's death. When Osiris was murdered by his brother, she roamed the world seeking his remains and shed so many tears the Nile flooded.[124]   In the weeping Cinderella, Bayley sees the long-suffering Isis, while Osiris is "the beautiful prince with the godlike face." He also lays out several parallel texts between *The Song of Songs* and *The Burden of Isis*.[125]

With her similarities to the Holy Virgin, it is understandable that Isis was the last of the Egyptian goddesses to yield to Christianity. In a way she lives on, clandestinely, through Mother Mary. A sea deity, Isis set sail for France where one syllable of her name provided a suffix for many French towns. The most notable was Paris to which she became patroness until the Virgin took over this title plus many of her shrines and temples.[126]

The Assyro-Babylonian equivalent of Isis, dating from at least the previous millennium, was Ishtar, known to the Sumerians as Innana and the Canaanites as Astarte, whose connection with Cinderella cannot be elaborated here. Amongst her titles were: Mistress of Heaven and Earth, Creatress of Wisdom, Star of Splendour, Ishtar of the Stars.[127] As Zarpanit, she signified 'silver' and 'shining.'[128] The syllables 'ish' and 'tar' are said to mean 'light' and 'daughter.'[129] Reputedly, her father was the moon-god, Sin, whose name finds a distant echo in Cinderella.[130] Fickle as the moon, Ishtar was a temple harlot; one figure represents her naked with rays round her head and a crescent beneath her feet. Yet she was the wife *par excellence*, Mother of the Gods and Mother of Men, often depicted suckling a child. As Ninharsag, she wore the same horned headdress as Hathor; her holy milk nourished kings. Creatrix of All Things and Queen of the Dust, she was also entitled Mistress of the Field "who causes verdure to spring forth."[131]

Ishtar's importance as a vegetation goddess originated in her passionate relationship with the shepherd-god Tammuz to whom she was virgin-mother-wife-sister. The Shulamite's lover, too, was a shepherd.[132] Whether Solomon came to her in that guise, was part of a triangle or eventually supplanted him is a matter of conjecture.[133] Whatever her status, the Bride was certainly a lover of nature.[134] Cinderella's association with nature was stronger. Trees bowed down so that only she could pluck their fruit; sheep and cattle conferred special favours on her.

Ishtar's love, or that of her sister Allutu, Queen of the Underworld, occasioned Tammuz' death. Grief stricken, Ishtar resolved to retrieve him. During her descent into the Underworld she was obliged, at each gate, to cast off part of her magnificent clothing. She came before her sister crouched and stripped bare, as were Sumerians for the grave. Tried by seven judges and executed, Ishtar's body was strung on a peg, soon to putrify.[135]   In this sequence we can see the lethal forces ranged against the heartbroken Cinderella, whose loss of soul is vividly pictured when she is concealed in a corpse's skin.[136] We may also see the road to Calvary, the stripping of garments and the hanging on a tree. Cinderella was wise enough to leave the prince a clue when she disappeared into the darkness; Ishtar took a similar precaution in letting her destination be known. Help came in the form of Uddushu-Namir who sprinkled her with the water of life.[137]   Nowadays, Jesus' capacity to give life to the dead is taken over by statues of the Black Virgin, who specialises in still-born children and unbaptised babies.[138]

This theme of birth and death, of the vegetative cycle, became ritualised in an annual sacred marriage between the king and a temple prostitute, representing Ishtar. With their intercourse, Tammuz is figuratively enlivened and the crops flourish. Could the Israelites have been influenced by such a practice? The liturgical interpretation of *The Song of Songs* answers in the affirmative, seeing the book as a collection of songs taken over from such a pagan ceremony.[139] *The Song* certainly abounds with fertility symbols: wine, grapes, date palms, pomegranates, raisins and mandrakes. Moreover, it celebrates a wedding having a dance reminiscent of a Syrian custom where the bride dances with a naked sword during week-long festivities that see her beauty extolled; and *wasfs*, poems bearing a similarity to *The Song of Songs*, hailing her and the groom 'queen' and 'king.'[140]

Since uninhibited licentiousness characterised fertility cults, moralists were quick to object to any ancestral link with *The Song of Songs*: "It is inconceivable that a work of such origin should be in the canon."[141] Rabbi Akiva's position is interesting. While fighting for its inclusion, he restricted its use to the Passover and banned it from the very event *The Song* celebrates — a banquet.

Theories regarding the origin of *Cinderella* are relevant in this context. Some hold the story is a detritus Dawn or seasonal myth, perhaps based on a spring festival. An alternative hypothesis is that the ball stems from the bride-show, a custom where the king selects a partner from assembled candidates. Not only was each girl's face and stature examined but 'the sandal on the foot' was measured.[142] More may now be read into the Shulamite's sandalled feet, a shoe being "the symbol of the fruitful female organ itself."[143]

The Virgin's position is crucial in determining attitudes towards pagan marriage festivals. The urge to uphold her purity places Christianity in a unique position for she is also the ultimate symbol of fertility. Fertility, like all creative acts, tends to be self diffusive, to overspill, go beyond bounds.[144] The Great Mother can be generous to the point of promiscuity. The Shulamite has been seen as a saucy Damsel;[145] Cinderella is a Hearth Cat; both Isis and Ishtar were sacred harlots. Perhaps, therefore, the Virgin's extramarital impregnation, so initially disturbing to Joseph, is not a strange anomaly but a spiritualised manifestation of this phenomenon.

The problem for modern women is how to embody the feminine principle and secure equality in a society driven by male values. Perera suggests that Ishtar's Descent offers a way of initiation. For some, the Black Virgin may provide a more acceptable model. If virginity is to have real significance for the vast majority of women, it must denote a state of mind. The psychological virgin, for Woodman, is she who is 'one-in-herself,' who confidently operates from her inner feminine reference point.[146] In so doing, she rescues her own child from whom she has been separated through prostitution to others' values. This child is the abandoned Cinderella, rejected by a Lear-type father or patriarchally identified mother. Unjustly denigrated, she corresponds to the Virgin for whom there was no room at the inn. Nowadays, this aspect of the Virgin lives on in her blackened form, outcast like a gypsy.[147] Being one-in-herself ensures that reaching out to others does not entail the self-depletion that characterised the lowly Cinderella; rather it is an enrichment or amplification of the self.

Truth and Love yield Wisdom, according to ancient understanding. The twin circles appearing on the Vase of Wisdom may be taken as stylised breasts; one Alma Mater is pictured with two streams of milk flowing from her. Within an uroborous, this pair may also be portrayed as two storks representing 'filial piety.'[148] They complement each other like brother and sister, like the Shulamite, Isis, Ishtar and their soul-mates. According to Jungian psychology, the fourth stage of anima development takes the form of a wisdom figure who becomes a man's spiritual guide.[149] Such was the Gnostic Sophia, who was originally coexistent with God. But she became entangled in the world and her plight had to be relieved by the Great Light, Christ, who "emanated and descended to His own sister."[150] "Say unto wisdom 'You are my sister,' and call understanding your next of kin."[151] *Proverbs* also records: "Wisdom has built her house, she has hewn out seven pillars."[152] She appears in the name of Hathor, Hathor, House of Horus.[153] Bayley finds echoes of her in the Cinderella who, under interrogation by a prince anxious to determine her identity, answers to a query about where she lives: "In the house with the door." The female element in humans was regarded by mystics as a "house and wall of man, without whose binding and redeeming influence he would inevitably be dissipated and lost into the abyss."[154] Once again, hearth and home come into focus as do the Shulamite's words: "I am a wall."[155] The opening of her door has been mentioned. A further crossing of the paths of Cinderella and the Shulamite occurs in that flower of wisdom, the rose, and in the apple, tree of immortality-through-wisdom, for we read in *The Song*:[156]

I awakened you under the apple tree.
There your mother brought you forth;
There she who bore you brought you forth.

The apple tree was sacred to Venus who, through the Greek Aphrodite, we have met in Ishtar.

Finally, whether or not they were lovers, the Shulamite will always have a claim on wisdom for her name is the feminine version of Solomon, 'peace,' the fruit of Love and Truth.

When a unicorn lodges in a thicket, belief states that it can only be rescued by a pure virgin, Wisdom herself.[157] She is the essence of fertility, saying: "Whoever finds me, finds life ... all those who hate me love death."[158] Mary is the Seat of Wisdom but the Missal is quick to point out that Wisdom properly belongs to the Word. And so, as a "man's wisdom makes his face shine,"[159] Jesus' "face shone like the sun, and his clothes became as white as light"[160] at the transfiguration. Likewise Stephen was bathed in glory.[161] This is the aureole of the saints and for those who can see, it is no metaphor. The brilliance of Cinderella at the ball now conveys much more than a pretty girl. It has a profound meaning to which we are blinded by its intensity. Thus, Wisdom remains inscrutable. As Isis says: "I am that which is, has been, and shall be, and no man has lifted my veil."[162] Wisdom here is unmanifest and unrevealed.[163] Her veil is the virgin's curtain: she who has not yet known, who is in the dark, but is to be prized more than rubies and with whom none can compare.[164] Wisdom is unique — one-in-herself.

Tales entitled *Mary the Smutty Nosed*,[165] *Little Dirty Skin*[166] and *The Black Girl*[167] speak of the heroine's filthy condition and provide reason for her to be called *The Ugly Cinderella*.[168] Ugliness is the foil of beauty; together they demonstrate the extremes characteristic of fairy-tales.[169] Her often sooty appearance is due to the fire which takes its toll

even on the Red Indian Cinderella. Naturally brown, she is
disfigured by scarring from hot cinders pressed into her by a
wicked sister calling her Rough Faced Girl.[170] Occasionally,
this evil sister is given the derogatory name Brown or Swarthy
Maid,[171] but generally it is Cinderella who displays the
family's darker side. She is the scapegoat, the black sheep. In
an Irish tale, however, she is the progeny of a king and black
sheep, who is a woman by night.[172] Cinderella's step-mother
is not one who would sanction her dirty linen being washed in
public. She is the whited sepulchre. This interplay between
inner jealousy and outer facade, between shadow and persona,
is symbolised in one impossible task she set a Cinderella: to
wash a black handkerchief white and vice versa.[173] Often a
helpful animal completes such a task. In an unusual story, the
evil doers feed Cinderella a black cat. Outcast and failing to
die as intended, she gives birth to a black cat through whom she
is eventually saved.[174] The self-born motif is clear. In
another tale, the heroine's beauty, her fair white skin, results
from her drinking the milk of a black cow.[175]

   The Shulamite's swarthiness was likened to the black
goats' hair tents of Kedar, a word meaning 'black.' She was
also beautiful as the curtains of Solomon's palace.[176] Curtains may have a heavenly attribution;[177] they resemble a veil.
Consequently the covered Shulamite[178] is akin to the black,
veiled Isis. Germination takes place in darkness. Night, the
Mother of All Things, was portrayed with a starry veil and
holding two children, one black and one white. Carbon, black
in cinders and soot, is the "crystal clear water" of a dia-
mond.[179] Perhaps the Cinderella who meets her prince in a
black ball gown[180] radiates the "deep dazzling darkness" of
which a mystic speaks.[181] Lowly, she is black but beautiful:
redeemed, she is black and beautiful.

   For Cinderella black is: the night into which she
vanishes at midnight; the prince's pitch trap set the following
evening to catch her shoe; her melancholy, mourning, humility

and denigration; the alchemical *nigredo*, the terrible shadow and first stage of the transformative process; the gestating womb, the veil of mystery surrounding her identity; her latent resources and hidden wisdom.

Graves sketches three kinds of women: the domestic ideal of the veiled Vesta; the capricious Muse, White Goddess who sends men mad and inspires poets; and the Black Goddess who "promises a new pacific bond between men and women" in the certitude of love.[182] Perhaps that bond could extend to black and white, and others at odds. Surely she is the woman of Chaucer's *The Wife of Bath*? Sentenced to death for ravishing an innocent maiden, a lusty knight will be reprieved if he can answer the question: What do women want? After a year's fruitless searching, he comes upon an impecunious old hag who will impart the secret on a condition she will later reveal. He agrees but is utterly dismayed when, after being granted his life, he is required to honour the bargain: become her husband. When he baulks at the marriage-bed, she chides him asking: Would he not prefer an ugly, constant wife to a siren who would cuckold him? He may take his choice. Cornered, he lets the decision be hers and thereby she acquires mastery over him. Lifting the curtain, he is then confronted by a ravishing beauty who pledges complete faithfulness. Such a woman is unavailable to the man who has not suffered at the hands of the White Goddess, who has not been chastened by the flames of passion, who has not humbled his intellectual hubris.[183] The maiden of Chaucer's tale is the virginal Vesta. The hag is the 'corpse flesh' of serpent love, the leprous White Goddess; she is also the corpse-Cinderella and the girl whose inexplicable disappearance at the strike of twelve shatters the love-sick prince. The knight's transformed wife is the Black Goddess.

Finally we return to the grate, one of the most feminine of vessels. Herein lies the woman of D.H. Lawrence's dreams:[184]

I wish I knew a woman
who was like a red fire on the hearth
glowing after the day's restless draughts

and *The Mother* of Katherine Tynan's poem:[185]

I am the fire upon the hearth,
I am the light of the good sun.
I am the heat that warms the earth,
Which else were colder than stone.

And the Hearth-Cat Cinderella. Here is the nest of the self-born phoenix — one-in-herself like the pregnant virgin. Here Cinderella hides after fleeing the ball, once again as dark as death but radically different as she awaits her love. All these themes are interwoven in *The Hearth*.[186] In this poem, Graves pictures a worm turning chick, then dove, an ancient representation of Night. And he pities the man who has not nestled under her pearl grey wings, for how could he see when midnight strikes, dove become phoenix, or hale to some hilly stronghold:

Where an unveiled woman, black as Mother Night,
Teaches him a new degree of love
And the tongues and songs of birds?

Notes

1. *The Song of Songs*, 1:5. [hereafter *Song*]. I have taken the translation from the Douay Rheims version because the words and alliteration highlight the perspective of this paper. Other extracts in the paper are taken from whatever translation best expresses my point. For brevity,

these will not be listed.   In the 12 Bibles, published between 1611-1980, that I consulted the Hebrew *shachor* and *sheckarchoreth* (*Song* 1:6) are variously rendered: black, swarthy, brown, colour, Ethiop, dark, little dark; and *naveh*: beautiful, lovely, comely.   Cf. "Black am I and beautiful" in Marvin H. Pope, *Song of Songs* (New York: Doubleday, 1977), pp. 1, 291, 307-311, 321-322, where he discusses the adversative 'but' which appears in the Vulgate, *Nigra sum sed formosa*, but not in the Greek Septuagint, *melaina eimi (ego) kai kale*.   This point was discussed on Insights, 2FC Radio Australia, 11 February, 1990 by Cain Hope Felder in relation to black activism. I have been unable to locate or obtain details of his book *Troubling Biblical Waters, Blacks in the Bible*.   See note 169 below.

Verse and Psalm numbering follows the Revised Stan dard Version.

2. Harold Bayley, *The Lost Language of Symbolism* (London: Williams & Norgate, 1912 [reprinted 1974], I, pp. 179, 215.

3. Ibid., I, p. 181.

4. Shame and nakedness are discussed by Francis Landy, "The Song of Songs and the Garden of Eden," *Journal of Biblical Literature*, 98 (1979), 513-528, esp. pp. 522, 524, 526.   His thesis is that *The Song* is an inversion of the *Genesis* Garden of Eden.   Features of both books are to be found in *Cinderella*.   See also Francis Landy, *Paradoxes of Paradise* (Sheffield: Almond Press, 1983), pp. 219-226, 235, 253-4, 263-4, 340n69, 342n88, 354n155.

5. *Song* 1:6.

6. Ibid. The Ryrie Study *Bible* describes her mother's sons as step- rather than half-brothers. Cf. Pope, op. cit., 322-3.

7. Marian Roalfe Cox, *Cinderella* (London: Folklore Soc., 1893), p. 521, refers to a Russian story reported by Veselovsky, *Slavyanskiya, Skazaniya o Solomonye i Kitovrasye* (Petersburg, 1872), pp. 110-111. Cox is cited by Bayley, op. cit., I, p. 179.

8. Ean Begg, *The Cult of the Black Virgin* (London: Routledge & Kegan Paul, 1985), p. 29.

9. Ibid., pp. 7, 21, 49, 107. Cf. Pope, op. cit., p. 313.

10. Ibid., p. 29.

11. Ibid., p. 26.

12. *New Catholic Encyclopedia* (New York: McGraw Hill, 1967), IX, 352-6. The spiritual maternity of Mary was first alluded to by Sixtus IV in 1477; it covers the baptised who form a Mystical Body, i.e., the Church.

13. Begg, op. cit., p. 26.

14. Ibid., p. 200.

15. Ibid., pp. 2-3, 9-10.

16. *The Little Office of the Immaculate Conception.* Hymn for Nones.

17. *I Kings* 1:1-4, 15.

18. Sometimes called Shulammite or Shunammite, see: Matthew Black (Gen. ed.), *Peake's Commentary on the Bible* (London: Thomas Nelson, 1962), p. 473; Mierill Tenney, (Gen. ed.), *The Zondervan Pictorial Bible Dictionary* (Grand Rapids: Zondervan, 1967), pp. 5, 791; John McKenzie, *Dictionary of the Bible* (London: MacMillan, 1965), pp. 4, 810.

19. McKenzie, ibid., p. 810.

20. *Song* 6:13.

21. Isidore Singer (ed.), *Jewish Encyclopedia* (New York: Ktav Pub. House, 1901), XI, p. 314.

22. *Song* 2:1. Cf. ibid., 5:13; 7:2; Bayley, op. cit., II, pp. 229, 236.

23. *The New American Standard Bible* (1978) finds no sufficient reason to reject Solomon's authorship. *Peake's Commentary*, p. 468 states that there is nothing that would suggest Solomon's authorship. Carlo Suarès, *The Song of Songs ... deciphered according to the original code of the Qabala* (Berkeley: Shambala, 1972), pp. 7-8 is adamant that Solomon, "this pompous king, could not have written it because he was no cabalist, whereas *The Song* lies in the very heart of Qabala." It is for this reason that Rabbi Akiva, during the 1st century, insisted on it being placed in the canon, judging it to be the most holy of Scriptures, "the whole universe" not being "worth the day" *The Song* was given to Israel. The other great cabalistic work is *Genesis* which is interesting in view of note 4 above.

24. J.E. Cirlot, *A Dictionary of Symbols*, trans. Jack Sage (London: Routledge, 1971), p. 275.

25. George Ferguson, *Signs and Symbols in Christian Art* (New York: Oxford U.P., Galaxy Book, 1966), pp. 37-38, 96, 168.

26. Herbert Whone, *Church Monastery Cathedral* (Wiltshire: Compton Russell, 1977), pp. 144-145.

27. *Song* 1:6. While some interpret 'vineyard' as the Bride or her personal appearance, others take it to mean her body and hence a loss of virginity. See Pope, op. cit., pp. 326-328 for a summary and Morris Jastrow Jr. *The Song of Songs* (Philadelphia: J.B. Lippincott, 1921), p. 123 who takes the second position.

28. Cox, op. cit., pp. 331-333, Rosina. Cf. Bayley, op. cit., II, pp. 229, 234.

29. Ibid., p. 451, *Das Rösenmadchen*, a Hero tale. See also: a film *The Slipper and the Rose* and my own story *The Sandal and the Rose* in *Religious Traditions*, 11 (1988), 21-38. In my commentary on this entitled *Cinderella Returned* (in preparation) I discuss many topics that can only receive mention here.

30. Lindsay MacKay, *Cinderella and the Prince*, an operetta (London: Curwen, c. 1897) where the plot turns on a magic rose given the heroine by her fairy-godmother; Anna Brigitta Rooth, *The Cinderella Cycle* (Lund: Gleerup, 1951), pp. 18-19 where a magic rose tree bestows ball gowns; Cox op. cit., pp. 287, 297.

31. *Song* 2:2. Cf. *Ezekiel* 2:6; 28:24.

32. *Little Office* ... Hymn at Vespers.

33. Cox, op. cit., p. 314.

34. For a discussion of this passage in relation to Christ, see
    Matthew Henry's Commentary on the whole Bible (?1725,
    [reprint Iowa Falls: World Bible Pub., n.d.]), III, 1061-
    1062.

35. Ferguson, op. cit., p. 34.

36. *Matthew* 6:29.

37. Whone, op. cit., p. 101.

38. *Song* 4:7.

39. Jastrow, op. cit., pp. 65-138; McKenzie, op. cit., pp.
    834-835; *New Am. Stand. Bible*; Peake, op. cit., 468-470;
    Pope, op. cit., pp. 34-36, 89-229 mention some or most
    of the allegoric, dramatic, typical, literal, mystical,
    dream, cultic, wedding week, lyric idyll and funeral feast
    conjectures with varying degrees of completeness.

40. Cited by Marion Woodman, *The Pregnant Virgin*
    (Toronto: Inner City Books, 1985), p. 54. In this book
    she argues for an enfranchisement of and reconnection
    with the body.

41. Robert Graves, *Mammon and the Black Goddess* (London:
    Cassell, 1965), pp. 147-148, 164-165. Cf. Begg, op.
    cit., p. 71; Gertrude Jobes, *Dictionary of Mythology,
    Folklore and Symbols* (New York: Scarecrow Press,
    1962), I, p. 765 Hestia; II, pp. 1647-1648 Vesta.

42. Cox, op. cit., p. 421; Bayley, op. cit., I, pp. 225-226.

43. Cox, op. cit., pp. xxv-xxvi classifies stories with this
    motif as Type B. Rooth, op. cit., pp. 14-15, 19-20 as
    Type B1. See notes 95-97 below.

44. Graves, op. cit., p. 149.

45. Bayley, op. cit., I, pp. 194-195. For Cinderella as a manifestation of divine virtues, modelled on certain exemplary 16th century Christian converts rather than arising from an indigenous folk base, see: Chieko Irie Mulhern, "Cinderella and the Jesuits An *Ontogizōshi* Cycle as Christian Literature," *Monuments Nipponica*, 34 (1979), 409-447. The author argues that the tales were written by Jesuits between 1600-1614 as a subtle method of proselytising in face of persecution. Substituting for sermons, their genre nevertheless has connections with Buddhist sermons (pp. 432, 439). Interestingly, the first record of Cinderella in Europe is in a sermon in Strasburg during 1501, see: Alan Dundes, (ed.), Editorial Comment in *Cinderella A Folklore Casebook* (New York: Garland, 1982), p. 4.

46. Begg, op. cit., pp. 2, 6-8, 55, 85; Pope, op. cit., p. 312.

47. R.D. Jameson, "Cinderella in China" in Dundes, op. cit., pp. 76, 85 (71-97); Photeine P. Bourboulis, "The Bride-Show Custom and the Fairy-Story of Cinderella," ibid., pp. 107, 108 (98-109).

48. *Song* 1:8, 5:9, 6:1.

49. Ibid., 6:8.

50. Ibid., 5:2, 6:9.

51. *Luke* 1:38, 48.

52. Ibid., 2:7.

53. Ibid., 1:28, 42.

54. *Matthew* 20:16; *Psalms* 136:23, 138:6.

55. Bourboulis, op. cit., pp. 103-105.

56. *Song* 7:1.

57. Bayley, op. cit., I, p. 180.

58. John Venard, ed., *The Spiritual Canticle of St. John of the Cross* (Sydney: E.J. Dwyer, 1980), p. 214.

59. It is quite common for the heroine in the Cycle to be a king's daughter, as expressed in the title *The Beautiful Princess* in Cox, op. cit., pp. 75, 365. Cf. Mulhern, op. cit., pp. 444-445.

60. Begg, op. cit., p. 17; McKenzie op. cit., p. 212 states that Egyptians called their country *Kemet*, 'the black land.'

61. Origen, *The Song of Songs Commentary and Homilies*, trans. & annotated by R.P. Lawson (London: Longmans, Green, 1957), p. 331n57. For Origen's discussion of Ethiopian, see pp. 92-92, 95-98, 103-104, 106-107.

62. Ibid., p. 21.

63. *Genesis* 16:1-15.

64. *Numbers* 12:1.

65. Origen, op. cit., p. 110 & n.

66. Ibid., p. 107.

67. *Song* 8:5. Knox points out that the italicised words appear in the Septuagint but not the Hebrew text.

68. *Song* 6:10. Cf. 6:4; Bayley op. cit., I, pp. 167, 171. Cf. Begg, op. cit., p. 19. When the final line is added: "terrible as an army set in battle array" the whole verse becomes the antiphon in the Catena Legionis of the Legion of Mary. For a discussion and translation: "Who is she gazing forth like the morning star, Fair as the moon, Bright as the sun, Awe-inspiring like these great sights?," see: Robert Gordis, "The root רגל in the Song of Songs," *Journal of Biblical Literature*, 88 (1969), 203-204.

69. Cox, op. cit., p. 190.

70. Ibid., pp. 169, 241, 255, 257, 259, 335. See ibid., p. 480n12 for her likening of this to an aureole. Rooth, op. cit., p. 17.

71. Ibid., p. 365.

72. Ibid., p. 164. Cf. Ibid., pp. 277, 278, 335, 360, 431, 478n7. Angel or heaven help, ibid., pp. 300, 326, 414, 434.

73. Origen, op. cit., pp. 108, 110-111, 331n60.

74. *Psalm* 45:13-14. Robert Graves, *The Song of Songs* (London: Collins, 1973), p. 12 sees this *Psalm* as the source of *Song* 6:9. Cf. note 49.

75. *Revelation* 12:1. Cf. Bayley, op. cit., I, p. 232; Begg, op. cit., p. 100.

76. *New Cath. Encylop.*, IX, p. 354, Cf. p. 342.

77. A Religious of C.S.M.V. (ed. & trans.), *Saint Bernard*

on the Song of Songs (London: A.R. Mowbray, 1952), p. 77.

78. *Song* 2:5. King James.

79. Ibid. Jerusalem.

80. Giambattista Basile, "The Cat Cinderella," in Dundes, op. cit., p. 10.

81. Ibid., p. 11n15.

82. Cox, op. cit., p. xxv & summaries, pp. 2, 7, 19, 24, 33, 40, 44, 47, 90, 437, 441, 443, 445. Rooth, op. cit., Appendix III, IV, VI, VIII, IX, X, XIII, XIV, XV.

83. *Luke* 1:29.

84. *John* 2:1-11.

85. Bayley, op. cit., I, p. 183.

86. Ibid., I, pp. 174-175. Cf. ibid., pp. 254-255; Cox, op. cit., p. 349.

87. *Song* 5:2-7.

88. Ibid., 5:8. Cf. ibid., 2:5.

89. Ibid., 6:13. Cf. Bayley, op. cit., I, p. 156.

90. Cox, op. cit., p. xxvi where she states the motif is found in her Types B, C & D for summaries of which, see pp. 53-121.

91. Begg, op. cit., pp. 13, 187.

92. Cited by Bayley, op. cit., I, p. 231.

93. *Song* 4:9. Cf. ibid., 4:10, 4:12, 5:1-2. The terms 'bro-
    ther' and 'sister' are variously related to Eastern mar-
    riages between siblings, signs of closeness, implications
    of chastity and sublimated incest desire, see: Jastrow, op.
    cit., p. 194n5; Landy (1979), pp. 523, 527; Landy
    (1983), pp. 70, 97-98, 101, 110-111, 116, 345n105;
    Pope, op. cit., pp. 480-481; Michael V. Fox, *The Song
    of Songs and the Ancient Egyptian Love Songs* (Madison,
    University of Wisconsin Press, 1985), pp. xii-xiii, 8n1,
    9nd, 12ng, 13 & nb, 136.

94. Bayley, op. cit., I, pp. 181-2, Cf. I, p. 243.

95. Cox, op. cit., p. 428. Cf. ibid., pp. 205-206 for virgin-
    ity test.

96. Ibid., pp. 365-366.

97. Ibid., pp. 53-79 for summaries. See: ibid., pp. 274-275
    where there is an unnatural brother.

98. Ibid., summaries pp. 80-86. Alan Dundes, "'To Love
    My Father All': A Psychoanalytic Study of the Folktale
    Source of *King Lear*," In Dundes, op. cit., pp. 229-244.

99. Rooth, op. cit., p. 112.

100. Bayley, op. cit., p. 112.

101. Bentley Layton (trans.), *The Gnostic Scriptures* (London:
    SCM Press, 1987), p. 80. Cf. Woodman, op. cit., p.
    121.

102. Erich Neumann, *The Great Mother*, trans. Ralph Manheim (London: Routledge & Kegan Paul, 2nd ed., 1963), pp. 3-11.

103. Woodman, op. cit., p. 14. Landy (1983), pp. 311-312 cites Rosemary Gordon on the mythical "coupling of women with death" as the price of giving birth. Pope, op. cit., 210-229 argues that the *Song* celebrates a funeral feast, love being the only conqueror of death (*Song* 8:6). It may be significant that the story of Psyche, a proto-Cinderella, begins with a bridal procession for her marriage to Death. Instead, alone and exposed on a crag, she is found by Eros and eventually becomes immortal.

104. For the vessel as the central symbol of the feminine, see Neumann, op. cit., pp. 39-54, and note 82 above for the cornucopian horn. Cf. Landy (1983), p. 63, 302n21.

105. Dating discussed by: Fox, op. cit., pp. 186-190; Pope, op. cit., 22-33.

106. Begg, op. cit., pp. 17, 50, 66, 143.

107. James Hastings (ed.), *Encyclopaedia of Religion and Ethics* (Edinburgh: T&T Clark, 1971 impr.), 7, pp. 434-436; Jobes, op. cit., 845-846.

108. Bayley, op. cit., I, p. 185.

109. Begg, op. cit., p. 62.

110. Bayley, op. cit., I, p. 233. Cf. note 75 above.

111. Jobes, op. cit., II, p. 1187. She depicts concentrated wisdom.

112. Begg, op. cit., pp. 13, 62.

113. Ibid., pp. 32, 166, 259. Cf. ibid., pp. 28, 98-99, 196, 197, 239.

114. Ibid., pp. 25, 62, 104, 133.

115. For comments on Rabin's view that the *Song's* origin might lie in Tamil love poetry, see: Fox, op. cit., p. xxvi; Landy (1983), pp. 28, 283n31; Pope, pp. 27-33.

116. Cox, op. cit., p. 262. Cf. ibid., p. 188; Bayley, op. cit., I, pp. 105, 191, 193, 205.

117. Begg, op. cit., p. 46; Jobes, op. cit., I, p. 731.

118. Rooth, op. cit., pp. 15-16 where Types A1 & A11 are summarised.

119. *Song* 1:13; 4:5; 7:3, 7, 8; 8:10. The imagery of breasts and date palms is discussed by Landy (1983), pp. 48, 54, 74-78, 81-85, 93, 101, 114-116, 162, 301n16, 307n36. For wisdom linked to the breast, see Neumann, op. cit., Schema II between pp. 41-42.

120. Begg, op. cit., p. 63.

121. Jobes, op. cit., I, p. 846.

122. Bayley, op. cit., I, pp. 278, 280, 283, 284.

123. Robert Graves, *The White Goddess* (London: Faber & Faber, 1961), p. 337.

124. Jobes, op. cit., I, p. 845.

125. Bayley, op. cit., I, pp. 170-171, 179.

126. Begg, op. cit., pp. 64, 66-68.

127. Hastings (ed.), *Encyclop.*, 7, pp. 428-434.

128. Ibid., p. 428n5.

129. Bayley, op. cit., I, p. 283.

130. Ibid., pp. 272, 286-287.

131. Hastings (ed.), *Encyclop.*, 7, p. 430n2.

132. *Song* 1:7.

133. The Shepherd hypothesis is part of the Dramatic Theory, see, Pope, op. cit., pp. 136-137, 334.

134. *Song* 7:11-12.

135. Jobes, op. cit., I, pp. 844; Sylvia Brinton Perera, *Descent to the Goddess* (Toronto: Inner City Books, 1981), pp. 9-10, 21, 53, 63, 81-82.

136. Cox, op. cit., pp. 134, 196, 242. Cf. ibid., p. 226; Mulhern, op. cit., pp. 444-445.

137. Bayley, op. cit., I, pp. 176, 179.

138. Begg, op. cit., pp. 10, 172, 184, 188, 207, 224, 282.

139. Fox, op. cit., pp. xxvi, 204-205, 220-221, 239-242, 268-269, 287; Peake, op. cit., p. 469; Pope, op. cit., pp. 42, 81, 145-153, 210-212, 324, 361-362, 373, 419, 421-422, 491, 497.

140. *Song* 6:13-7:9. This passage is said to describe a dance: Peake, op. cit., p. 473; Pope, op. cit., pp. 601-607; McKenzie, op. cit., p. 835. Singing might accompany such dancing, e.g. the *wasf*, a descriptive song praising

the beloved's body: Fox, ibid., pp. 128, 232, 269-275, 329; Pope, op. cit., pp. 67-68, 142-144; Richard N. Soulen, "The *wasfs* of the Song of Songs and hermeneutic," *Journal of Biblical Literature*, 86 (1967), 183-190. Festivities may last a week: Pope, op. cit., pp. 141-145; Jastrow, op. cit., pp. 117-119.

141. Tenney, *Zondervan … Dict.*, p. 803.

142. Bourboulis in Dundas, op. cit., pp. 106-107. Cf. Cox, op. cit., p. 162, 'beauty test;' Mulhern, op. cit., pp. 410-423 'bridal contest.'

143. Jameson in Dundas, op. cit., p. 89. Cf. Pope, op. cit., pp. 110, 381.

144. Woodman, op. cit., p. 80.

145. Jastrow, op. cit., pp. 123, 125, 161. Cf. Pope, op. cit., p. 414.

146. Woodman, op. cit., pp. 9, 51, 81, 117.

147. Ibid., p. 122.

148. Baylcy, op. cit., I, pp. 10, 245, 268-272, 275. See also note 119 above.

149. Marie-Louise von Franz cited in Woodman, op. cit., p. 146.

150. *The Wedding Song of Wisdom* cited in Bayley, op. cit., I, p. 175.

151. *Proverbs* 7:4.

152. *Proverbs* 9:1.

153. Bayley, op. cit., I, p. 254.

154. Ibid., pp. 254-256; Cox, op. cit., p. 349. Cf. note 86 above.

155. *Song* 8:10. Cf. Ibid., 8:9.

156. Ibid., 8:5. Cf. ibid., 2:3,5. Cf. Bayley, op. cit., II, p. 251.

157. Graves (1961), p. 255. Cf. Graves (1973), p. 16.

158. *Proverbs* 8:35-36.

159. *Ecclesiastes* 8:1.

160. *Matthew*, 17:2. Cf. *Exodus* 34:29-30, 35 for Moses and note 70 above.

161. *Acts* 6:10, 15.

162. Bayley, op. cit., I, p. 168.

163. Ibid., pp. 197-198, 214; Begg, op. cit., pp. 143-144.

164. *Proverbs* 8:11.

165. Cox, op. cit., pp. 66, 274.

166. Ibid., pp. 86, 415. Cf. ibid., pp. 23, 273.

167. Ibid., pp. 8, 150, Chernushka.

168. Ibid., pp. 15, 210-211.

169. Max Lüthi, *The Fairytale as an Art Form and Portrait of Man*, trans. Jon Erickson (Bloomington, Indiana Univer-

sity Press, 1984), pp. 28-30, 36. Cf. notes 1, 5-6, 46 above and the tale (ibid., pp. 29-30) having features similar to some Cinderella stories, where the last and loveliest of three beautiful girls is to marry a prince. She is thrown into a well by a jealous Macedonian Gypsy girl who, in passing herself off as the heroine, explains the origin of her black face to the questioning   prince: "From the sun, Lord, it has burned me ..."

170. Idries Shah, "The Algonquin Cinderella," *World Tales* (Middlesex: Allen Lane/Kestrel, 1979), pp. 152-155.

171. Cox, op. cit., pp. 188, 203. Cf. ibid., 332.

172. Reidar Christiansen, "Cinderella in Ireland," *Béaloideas*, 20 (1950), 96-107, p. 102.

173. Avelina Gil, "Mayyang and the Crab: a Cinderella variant," *Philippine Quarterly of Culture & Society* 1 (1973), 26-32, pp. 28, 30.

174. Cox, op. cit., p. 308.

175. Ibid., p. 322.

176. *Song* 1:5.

177. *Psalm* 104:2; Bayley, op. cit., I, p. 215; Bernard, op. cit., p. 76.

178. *Song* 1:7, 4:1, 8, 5:7, 6:7.

179. Jung cited by Cirlot, op. cit., pp. 57-58.

180. Cox, op. cit., pp. 203, 285. Cf. ibid., p. 284.

181. Henry Vaughan, *Silex Scintillans*, "The Night," cited by Bayley, op. cit., I, p. 215.

182. Graves (1965), p. 164.

183. Graves (1965), p. 164.

184.   *I Wish I knew a Woman* cited by Woodman, op. cit., p. 142.

185. Cited by Bayley, op. cit., I, p. 265.

186. Graves (1965), pp. 163-164.

GODDESS CONSCIOUSNESS AND SOCIAL REALITIES: THE 'PERMEABLE SELF'[1]

Winnie Tomm

Introduction

Goddess consciousness presupposes experience of Goddess presence. In an attempt to relate experience and theory, I describe some of my own encounters with Goddess presence. My intention is to open up space for new knowledge. I have chosen to employ this method in order to contribute to a developing form of discourse which reflects women's religious experiences that are shaped by Goddess imagery. Hopefully this approach will facilitate new possibilities with respect to women's participation in the symbol-making process of our social and cultural evolution. If we accept that knowledge is both experiential and reflective, then all knowledge must be seen as personal knowledge. It is assumed in this paper that knowledge is situated within a consciousness affected by prior sensations and ideas. My own ideas of Goddess consciousness are informed by vivid experiences infused with female images and symbols.

The essay is divided into three parts. Part I is about religious experience as a criterion for knowledge and a motivator of social action. It includes references to my own experiences of Goddess presence. Part II is about sexuality, the 'individual,' and social contracts. It explores ways in which male sexuality defines the individual and how the male paradigm shapes civic society and the private lives of women and men. Part III discusses ways in which Goddess consciousness removes the assumption of exclusive ontological normativeness of male sexuality with respect to humanity in general. Female sexuality is given an independent status. It is argued that Goddess presence contributes toward a social and cultural transformation that is guided by a disposition toward mutual authority between "permeable selves." In Goddess symbology, as discussed in the paper, female nature is not the "other" form of human nature. It is not a variation of the central, male-imaged notion of humanity, grounded in God symbolism. In Goddess imagery, the female is "subject." She is free of the circumscribed ontological status prescribed for her in biblical history, within the 'God the Father' (patriarchal) model.[2] I maintain that Goddess consciousness propels a woman beyond the social roles prescribed by a patriarchal model of human nature and beyond the corresponding self-definitions which women internalize in patriarchy. A central feature of Goddess empowerment is a woman's claim over her own sexuality, which is a matter of both private and public concern.

A presupposition which guides this exploration is that Goddess consciousness motivates social action toward a more egalitarian social evolutionary model. I experience Goddess presence as integrative. This is similar to the experiences of others.[3] Social actions which are motivated by such experiences would, if one is consistent, be of an integrative nature. In other words, if those experiences constituted the major underlying intentionality of social action, then the social evolutionary process would more likely be characterised by cooperation rather than domination.

Part I: Religious Experience

In my view, religious experience is continuous with ordinary social experience. The two dimensions are mutually informative. Moral passion is likely to arise within a consciousness informed by integrative Goddess presence. Goddess and social consciousness are coextensive through shared principles of connectedness. Religious experience is seen as an important constitutive of both knowledge and action. The effectiveness of moral passion, which fuels social consciousness, relies on a coherence between beliefs about social justice and actions which facilitate it. Beliefs which are grounded in striking experiences of connectedness, e.g., religious experiences, tend to be passionate and move one to action. Knowing and acting are then virtually inseparable. Goddess consciousness, in this context, means knowing and acting in ways that connect to Goddess presence, experienced as an integrative reality.

Religious experience is scorned by atheists, doubted by skeptics, or simply reduced to psychological and/or social explanations by others. In our culture it is often ignored as irrelevant (or confounding) in the materialistic pursuit of success. For others, however, religious experience is the major source of personal agency. It is the source of centeredness of both eros and agapē — passion and compassion. For them, religious experience simultaneously strengthens self-respect/self-love (eros) and respect for the well-being of others/benevolence (agapē). It is this latter view that is reflected in this paper.

Consciousness of one's own strengths develops through exercising these capacities in relation to others. This account of agency is not new. Anyone who has vicariously experienced the life of Francis of Assisi, or has been temporarily lifted out of individual isolation by Martin Buber's "I-Thou" discussions, or has glimpsed Spinoza's "love of God" and his blissful intuition of cosmic causal interrelatedness, to cite a few examples, knows something of the metaphysical and ontological connectedness to which I am referring. All of these individuals, and many more of similar persuasion, inspired my consciousness and social participation.

Three years ago something happened that took me beyond the state of consciousness informed by these inspirational men. What I experienced was Goddess presence. It was unexpected and initially very foreign to me. It took some time before I was able to integrate the experience and to feel comfortable enough to share it with others. I do not regard Goddess consciousness as something that is incompatible with God consciousness, especially when the latter is of the nature of 'God as Spirit.' It is, however, incompatible with the 'God the Father' paradigm, when the latter does not allow for the kind of authority that women have who encounter Goddess presence. The 'God the Father' model has contributed to an evolutionary process guided by an intentionality reflected in the actions of conquering warrior-kings and citizens. Our notion of 'individual' has arisen in conjunction with the patriarchal model of God. 'Individual' is associated with the male, whose identity is defined in terms of ownership of property and/or supreme rational capacities (e.g., Locke and Descartes). Strong, dominating masculine traits have become our model for humanity, which is a male-centered model. The consequences of the warrior-king model with respect to the imposition of male sexuality on social contract theory will be discussed in Part II.

The 'God as Spirit' model, like the Goddess paradigm, is one of mutual authority and expansiveness. Helen Luke suggests that *spirit* means that "the true meaning is glimpsed by us only through the kind of experience that can never be rationally explained in words. Only the images which perennially emerge from the unconscious of humankind may convey in a symbol the power of the spirit" (1989:5). She says that spirit is "predominantly used on every level and without any moral connotation to express that which brings about a transformation" (p. 6). Goddess consciousness entails the transformative power of the spirit, experienced directly through female images.

Three years ago I returned to a place in the mountains which I often enjoyed because of its beauty and peacefulness. I have since come to call it the 'sacred place.' 'Sacred' means empowering. That particular location is empowering for me. It is a clearing in the mountains from which one can look out into a confluence of mountains, trees, and rivers. They converge in a way that is symbolic of the peaceful integration of nature. As a kind of tranquility settled throughout me, the image of three women's heads attached by a common bosom emerged in my consciousness. The image seemed to be 'located' between a particular peak on which I had been focused and where I was sitting. I experienced looking at the image as well as listening to the three women speak directly to me. One woman was young, one was middle-aged, and the other was old.

It was the old one who was the most present to me. It is not clear why I knew she was old. She did not have any wrinkles. Her head was covered by a wrap so I could not see the color of her hair. Yet there is no doubt that she was old. I now believe that I knew she was old because of the intenstity of her energy. From an American Indian perspective, Paula Gunn Allen states "The old ones were empowered by their certain knowledge that the power to make life is the source and model for all ritual magic and that no other power can gainsay it. Nor is that power really biological at base; it is the power of ritual magic, the power of Thought, of Mind, that gives rise to biological organisms as it gives rise to social organizations, material culture, and transformations of all kinds — including hunting, war, healing, spirit communication, rain-making, and all the rest...." (1989:27). If women are perceived as vitalizers, then their power increases with age, through participation in the transformative power of relatedness. This is true for men as well. Those who give birth to others, either biologically or socially, and enliven them through relationships increase their

own vitality through time. The vital energy of the old woman
was vivid in my consciousness.

Although I was drawn mostly to the old woman's
presence, the voice which I associate with the image was
expressed by all three at once. They requested that I "come to
their bosom" and said they would "take care of me." My
initial response was minimal. I had no doubt, however, about
what I had "heard" or "seen." It was a foreign experience,
though, which required time to assimilate. There was virtually
no coherence between it and other conscious experiences of
mine.

I was affected by the experience but not disturbed, nor
greatly motivated to integrate it. I did not expect anything
more. An hour later, however, the image re-emerged. The
same experience was repeated, with greater reception and
response on my part. I felt their presence in a more powerful
way and I felt myself inclining toward them. There was a
definite interaction which left me more energetic and expansive.
Then the image retreated and I was alone, but not as alone as
before.

The image returned a third time, about two hours later,
and the same words were part of the experience. The presence
of the image came into my consciousness in a very full way.
I experienced myself going to "their" bosom and being wholly
embraced by the three-in-one. At the same time I was fully
present to myself, standing in the clearing on the side of a
mountain. I was integrated into "them" simultaneously as I was
integrated in myself. The continuum among the three-in-one,
on the one hand, and between me as an identifiable individual
and as part of them, on the other, was undeniable. The reality
was a process of interaction, without distinctive boundaries, yet
with distinctive participants.

As a result of that experience, I have come to know
myself as a 'permeable self.' I am identifiable but not separate.
I am permeable, but not soluble. (I shall discuss the notion of

'permeable self' more fully in the section on the self in Part II). Following the third experience, I went down the mountain knowing myself in a new way. I was together. Together with the maiden (potentiality), the mother (creativity), and the old woman (wisdom) aspects of Goddess presence, both immanently (personally) and transcendently (as Other). From that time onward, Goddess presence has informed both my consciousness and actions. The social-political and psychological implications of Goddess experiences will be elaborated on in Part III.

Since that afternoon in the mountains when I first encountered the Goddess, I have had two other increasingly powerful experiences. I now live with a Goddess consciousness. Although it has been 'normalized' for me, as well as for many others, it is considered suspect in our society. Biblical history has given us a heritage of thirty-five hundred years filled with suspicion toward autonomous (self-determining) female power. The journey toward legitimizing independent female power is long and arduous. The first steps are often the most difficult because the signposts are scarce and are difficult to comprehend when they do appear.

My most recent powerful experience with the Goddess occurred six months ago. I was in the mountains, but in a different location. The experience lasted for about half an hour. The basic images consisted of a thin sheath of white energy or light; the same three-in-one image; a red, ocean-like wave of energy; and a thin, black snake about eighteen inches long. There remains for me a great deal of discovery about the meaning of that awe-filled half-hour. I feel both very small and huge when I recall it. After the experience was over I knew that something significant had taken place but was unsure how to give meaning to it. I knew, though, that it had pushed me forward into a new relationship within myself and with the rest of the world. The images dynamically related energy, the earth, and me in a way that is not describable because of the categorical nature of language. The limitations of any linguistic description of such an experience are apparent. Attempts to describe it according to the interpretive frameworks that we usually employ (such as various psychological, sociological, biological, or philosophical explanations) necessarily reduce it to a more static and less powerful experience than it was. Since then my thoughts, feelings, and actions have been affected by the integrative experiences of universal and personal energy. Some meaning has been given to it through discussion with colleagues who specialize in the study of archetypal images. Undoubtedly, further study will facilitate greater discovery of the meaning of that experience. I remain open to learning more about it and possibly to writing more explicitly about it.

In light of the widespread skepticism in Western religious traditions toward religious experiences in general and the antagonism toward Goddess reverence in particular, due to the negativity toward independent female sexuality, it is unlikely that one would be taken seriously by many when writing about encounters with the Goddess. The weight of that skepticism and antagonism has silenced many individuals with respect to discussion of religious experiences. It has silenced women in particular because of the exclusion and marginalization in our culture of female religious imagery that is independent of the traditional 'God the Father' paradigm. Because of my experiences, I would like to contribute to breaking the silence on Goddess-talk. During the past ten years the works of Paula Gunn Allen, Carol Christ, Mary Daly, Christine Downing, Naomi Goldenberg, Audre Lourde, Helen Luke, Nelle Morton, and Dhyani Ywahoo, among others, have opened new possibilities for "re-membering" ourselves as women with a normative ontological status. As a result of their pathbreaking efforts, more of us are leaving behind a disempowered consciousness. We are moving forward along newly constructed roads, leading to intersections in which we encounter each other through Goddess consciousness. The networks of interrelatedness expand through the connectedness of 'permeable selves.'

Goddess presence enlivens the reality of an individual's agency and facilitates awareness of self-determining powers. As a 'permeable self', one becomes increasingly open to and receptive of similar powers in others. It is reasonable, therefore, to suppose that Goddess consciousness would contribute toward social patterns which would be increasingly shaped by principles of mutual authority between women and men.

Part II: Sexuality, the 'Individual,' and Social Contracts

Goddess consciousness, in my experience, includes awareness of the connectedness of one's sexual energy with a more universal creative energy. It frees one from the restrictive patriarchal attitudes and practices toward female sexuality which shape our social contracts (both formal and informal). I am using 'sexuality' as a shorthand term for female embodied self-expression. It is an erotic and transforming power that one accepts as part of one's normal, personal attributes. Goddess consciousness includes acceptance of one's spiritual power through one's body. It includes being positively present to oneself as an embodied female before subjecting oneself to the influential gaze of another. Through Goddess presence, one acts from one's own agency rather than merely reacting to the desires and interests of another. The ability to sustain that presence depends on the openness and receptiveness of 'permeable selves.'

The power of transformation lies in such inclusive acceptance. Audre Lorde states "The erotic is a resource within each of us that lies in a deeply female and spiritual plane, firmly rooted in the power of our unexpressed or unrecognized feeling.... [in our society women] have been taught to suspect this resource, vilified, abused, and devalued...." (1989: 208). She says "The erotic is a measure between the beginnings of our sense of self and the chaos of our strongest feelings. It is an internal sense of satisfaction to which, once we have experienced it, we know we can aspire. For having experienced the fullness of this depth of feeling and recognizing its power, in honor and self-respect we can require no less of ourselves" (p. 209).

The erotic is differentiated from pornography. Eroticism includes feelings of powerful self-expression. Sexuality is grounded in the fullness of being. Self-expression is erotic when it is transformative for the subject. It is sacred and reveals the power of connection between the metaphysical creative, transformative power and the ontology of one's being. Pornography, on the other hand, reflects superficial sensations which contribute to the disempowerment of a person. Perceived differences between eroticism and pornography depend upon assumptions about the nature and purpose of women and men and their relations to each other. Female sexuality in our culture has shaped women's social realities much differently than male sexuality has shaped men's realities. I shall turn now to some ways in which the dominant-subordinate social relations of the sexes are shaped by the assumption of male sexual dominance.

For the most part, women's sexuality has been problematic throughout biblical history. Distinctions between respectable and disreputable women have revolved around women's sexual relations with men. Social relations of the sexes have been shaped by prescriptions concerning the expressions of women's sexuality. As Riane Eisler (1987) has demonstrated, the social relations of the sexes is the primary thread which connects the patterns of social evolution. From the perspective of a religious understanding of human nature, theories of social evolution assume some form of spiritual development. In the biblical history with which we are familiar, there has been considerable tension between attitudes towards women's sexuality and notions about living righteously (i.e., in a right relation to God).

Much of the tension has resulted from qualities attributed to God which have very little to do with embodiment, female or male. Another cause of tension is the close association of men with God-like attributes of omnipotence and omniscience and women with the nonGod-like attribute of materiality. Social relations of women and men have evolved along the lines of the distinction between immateriality and materiality. Women's sexuality has been the most explicit focus of women's materiality. The place of women in the social order has been largely defined according to the way in which their sexuality has been expressed. Marriage makes a woman's sexuality accept-able, motherhood sanctifies it. Women, as sexual beings, have been evaluated primarily with reference to men. Women's work, whether reproductive or otherwise, has been affected by the association of women with material embodiment and the view that their bodies are there most importantly to fulfill the expectations of men.

In light of the fact that women's sexuality independent from men has rarely been described positively, it is often difficult for women to experience their sexuality as a form of personal power which they are free to share or withhold. Marriage and prostitution are both determined to a large extent by an underlying sexual contract in which men's access to women's bodies is assumed as a male right (Pateman, 1988). In our society, we believe in individual freedom, including rights over one's body. Respect for privacy of property is intrinsic to our attitudes of respect for each other as individuals. Examination of the social relations between women and men indicates that there are different ways in which respect is granted to individuals according to whether they are female or male.

When we speak of individuality, ambiguity flourishes. A certain amount of anxiety is provoked with respect to the issues of autonomy and dependency. We have been conditioned to think in terms of either the separate or the soluble self, as

Catherine Keller (1986) has so eloquently discussed the matter. The paradigm of individuality that I wish to explore here is that of 'permeable self.' A 'permeable self' is one which is neither separated from nor dissolves into another, but rather expands through relationship. This notion is particularly poignant when considering the social relations of the sexes. It is a possible means of overcoming the pervasive associations of men as separate, self-sufficient, dominant individuals and women as soluble ingredients in the many recipes for heroic accomplishments of the masterful conquerors who become our cultural heroes.

I wish to focus on the importance of sex-specificity with respect to the notion of 'permeable self.' That is not to say that sexual difference is the only cause of constraint in social relations, but rather that it is the most fundamental one, in many situations. Economics, skin color, ethnicity, age, nationality, religion, disability, and many other attributes affect one's individuality and sociality. The focus here, however, is on the social implications of femaleness. I borrowed the term "sociality" from John Macquarrie (1983). It refers to the context of relatedness in which each individual is invariably situated. Although many social factors contribute towards individuality, I shall concentrate here on the issue of sexuality and the importance of sex-specific ontological claims with respect to the relation between individuality and sociality as they relate to the 'permeable self.'

'Permeable self' entails the notion of a free person who shares one's strengths through relatedness, ideally without differential social privileges or limitations. Freedom for women most importantly is freedom from the assumption of the male sex-right, from men's assumed right to women's bodies. It is freedom to enter into social relations which are not characterized by dominance and subordination merely because of gender ascriptions. That is, in positive terms, freedom to live with the awareness of a spiritual power that both reflects and enhances one's sexual independence through social relations.

Such freedom is coextensive with dependency, through receptivity of and responsiveness to others. Self-determination, in this view, is a social process occurring within a web of interactive relations among 'permeable selves.' Recognition of oneself as permeable, includes rejection of the notion of separate, self-sufficient self, as well as realization of one's unique, individual contributions to social relations. Permeability works in two directions: the self goes forth toward others and is, at the same time, affected by the coming forth of the other. Through permeability, expansion occurs. Self-sufficiency and control over another are obstacles to expansion of self and other. They lead to the existence of separate and soluble selves. The separate self requires the presence of a soluble self, rather than another separate self, in order to preserve autonomy in the face of conflicting interests. And these selves are never abstract individuals, as some theories assume.

Social contract theory, for example, depends on the claim that "individuals are naturally free and equal to each other, or that individuals are born free and born equal" (Pateman 1988: 39). Pateman claims that "The doctrine of natural individual freedom and equality was revolutionary precisely because it swept away, in one fell swoop, all the grounds through which the subordination of some individuals, groups or categories of people to others had been justified; or, conversely, through which rule by one individual or group over others was justified.... Rather than undermining subordination, contract theorists justified modern civil subjection" (pp. 39-40). Women, for example, were placed in the peculiar position of being free to subject themselves to conventional contracts which subjugated them.

To speak of autonomous individuals in the abstract has not been very helpful for women, not to mention various other

groups who are subjugated through employer-employee contracts. Pateman discusses the notion of individual as we find it
in John Locke. It is his definition which has dominated theories
of social contract and rules for social relations. Central to his
view is the claim that an individual is an owner of his own
person. He says "every Man has a Property in his own Person"
(Locke, *Two Treatises of Government*, Sect. 26). In his view
"all individuals are owners, everyone owns the property in their
capacities and attributes" (Pateman, 1988: 13). For Locke,
social contract is the genesis of political right. The free
individual is one who contracts freely in social relations to
exchange something he owns for something someone else owns,
including one's abilities. Everyone is supposedly equally free
to enter into such contracts.

   It is well known that the "everyone" for Locke is not
everyone. Political rights of free individuals were inseparable
from property rights. In Pateman's view, "political right
originates in sex-right" (p. 3), which is taken as a basis for
organizing social dominance and submission. Women, as
dependents, were part of what the autonomous individual
claimed to own. At the same time, women were considered
free individuals with respect to entering into marriage contracts.
Without taking institutionalized differences into account, social
contract theorists could argue that women, by their own
authority, chose to be subjugated by men through marriage.
The social contract theorists' argument is less plausible,
however, if one takes into account the social realities which
shape choice-making by alleged free individuals. Social
contract theory has institutionalized social inequalities in the
name of freedom. These social inequalities have been given
unquestionable authority from the 'God the Father' paradigm
discussed earlier. The conditions in which choices are made
have been determined largely according to the interests of
property holders who are granted an authority along the lines of
those attributed to warrior-kings, who derive their authority

from a magisterial God. Women's agency has been exercised mainly within the parameters of respectable relations with men as defined within the patriarchal paradigm. The "free" woman, independent of such circumscribed relations, is still often relegated to a disreputable status.

Personal authority is both taken and granted according to organizing principles of dominance and subordination. According to Pateman, women's subordination in all respects — including authoritative knowing — is grounded in the male sex-right. She claims that patriarchy derives from a hidden sexual contract, which privileges male access to women's bodies. Pateman calls that privilege the male sex-right: the original social contract. An original contract "explains why exercise of right is legitimate" (1988: 1). That contract initiates the patriarchal right which is "the power that men exercise over women" (1988: 1). Our social institutions, especially marriage, depend on the absence of female consciousness which gives women an authoritative status that is uncircumscribed by male legitimacy.

Every social contract since the original one has been underwritten by it, according to Pateman. If we look at the structuring of social relations throughout history (whether in social contracts, such as marriage or employer-worker arrangements, or informal social relations between the sexes) with the idea that they were shaped by the sexual contract, then we perceive the social relations of the sexes to be fundamentally characterized by dominance-subordination. A woman who enters into social relations between the sexes and who does not accept that hierarchical relation (either implicitly or explicitly) commits an act of insubordination. Feminist theory and the women's social movement constitute a collective act of insubordination.

Male sex-right is seen to be intrinsic to the rights of individuals in modern civil society. I reject Locke's notion of the individual. His account does, however, illustrate the more usual understanding of 'individual' and the concepts of autonomy and dependency. His view of the individual as a masculine free self and women as dependent upon those individuals signifies the dichotomous relation between autonomy and dependency in Western philosophy. For example, Peter Schouls paraphrases Locke's concept of 'individual': "Let us call an 'autonomous knowing being' a 'rational being'" (1980: 197). The free, property-holding individual is inseparable, in Locke's view, from the rational, authoritative individual. Male sexuality, financial privilege, and intellectual superiority have come to characterize the autonomous individual who is portrayed as the separate self. All other kinds of selves are soluble, in this account of the separate, self-sufficient 'individual.'

Feminists have understandably attempted to avoid the use of the terms 'individual' and 'autonomy.' Some feminists have also been very exercised about the positive value of dependency as a mode of connectedness rather than as a clinging vine syndrome manifested through nonage persons (e.g., C. Gilligan and N. Noddings). There are others who have done significant work on the inclusiveness of autonomy and dependency (e.g., M. Belenky *et al.*, S. Bishop Hill, C. Gould, C. Keller, G. Lloyd, N. Scheman, and S. Wendell).

When autonomy and dependency are viewed as polarities within a holistic view of interrelatedness (see Tomm, 1987), they can be understood to reflect the permeability of the self. The vitality of each participant increases through interaction. It is important, however, when discussing individual freedom that the notion of individual is relevant to actual individuals, who are normally either female or male. In contract theory, at least, the term 'individual' acquired a meaning which made it primarily apply to men. It is that understanding which continues today to influence our views about what an individual can or cannot do with respect to contracting social relations with others. These views are not unrelated to Locke.

Locke's notion of a free individual included the view that the person owned his own abilities and capacities. That is, a man stands apart from what is, from a common sensical point of view, taken to be part of himself, namely his abilities and functions: which means that he can own parts of himself in the same way that he can own a house. For Locke, women rarely entered into contracts. When they do so today, they tend to do so on the Lockean model. A consequence is that they feel justified in selling parts of their bodies, or services rendered by parts of their bodies, as if those parts and services are independent from themselves as persons.

Men do that as well when they enter the work of prostitution but they cannot do that with respect to reproduction. Their seed is separated from their bodies, whereas women's wombs are not. To enter into a surrogacy contract is to enter into the sale of one's person, in the same way as entering into a prostitution contract is. The way in which each is made to resemble other employment contracts, where a so-called free individual agrees to sell her or his labour for wages, is that a person's capacities are seen to be separate from the person.

Pateman presents the same argument regarding selling one's labor power for wages. Labor power is capacity. Therefore it is part of the self and cannot be separated from the person. Self-alienation occurs when one's labor or the product of one's labor is disconnected from the enlivenment of the self. There is no growth through meaningless work. The self is diminished. The 'permeable self' is enhanced through empowerment and is diminished through disempowerment. Social contracts theoretically protect each partner, but in practice they often are an exchange of obedience for protection. It is a misconception to describe the employment contract as an occasion in which two free individuals enter into an agreement based on universal principles of equality. The social inequalities which determine the nature of the contract minimize the possibility for equality. It is more aptly described as a contract in which there is an exchange of obedience for protection between more and less socially privileged persons.

As mentioned earlier, according to Pateman, underlying every social contract, hidden from analysis, there is the sexual contract. The sexual contract between men and women is derived from the assumed natural male sex-right: access to women's bodies. That assumed natural right became a civil right. Pateman argues that the original social contract was the sexual contract, giving power to men over women's bodies in a way that women do not have over men's bodies. The original crime, in her view, was not that of overthrowing the primal father by the sons, as Freud and others have described, but rather the sexual conquest of women by men: in metaphorical terms, by the primal father, the archetypal patriarch.

Pateman distinguishes between fraternal patriarchy and paternal patriarchy. Paternal patriarchy predates fraternal patriarchy, which developed with social contracts and civic government in which "the construction of sexual difference as political difference is central to civil society." In paternal patriarchy, political right was natural and political power was paternal. Kings were fathers and fathers were kings. Father-right, masculine sex right, and conjugal rights were all closely connected. Pateman claims that paternal, patriarchal right was preceded by the male sex-right. Reproduction was a necessary prerequisite for father-right to emerge. Later on, when the sons overthrew the father, a new kind of patriarchy emerged: fraternal patriarchy, to replace the paternal paradigm. The civic brotherhood would agree to operate cooperatively as free individuals among themselves, according to universal rules of justice and rights. The most basic right that each of the brothers in the fellowship had was access to individual women. They agreed to share women according to rules of dispersion, namely marriage contracts and incest taboos. Males' morality organized the place of female sexuality in the fraternity. Some women would be available to all, namely those who did not belong to any man in particular. They would be the disreputable ones, while those whose identity was circumscribed by their relation to a particular man would be respectable. A man without a woman was to be pitied and a man with another man's woman was to be punished. The rules for the social relations of the sexes were established through the male sex-right of the brotherhood of free individuals, the citizens of the emerging civil society. The social authority of men reflected the authority of God the Father and, conversely, it was reflected in that paradigm. God the Father was the dominant image of ultimate power while social power was (is) located in male imagery.

Historically, women remained largely outside civil society as well as separate from the holy order of the fathers of the church. They were located in the private household sphere, protected from other men by their husbands, and introduced to God the Father through the priests and male ministers. If they participated in civil (public) contracts it was through their significance as a daughter or wife of a patriarch. Their social power was closely connected to their "chastity" as defined by their male relatives. It was a derived power (see Tomm, 1990). Their vulnerability under the male sex-right was never far beneath the presentation of the socially powerful image they may have projected through their associations with men of achievement. Today the social relations of the sexes are not so much different.

Women are citizens of the public sphere and are free individuals with respect to entering into social contracts. It still remains a fact, however, that the sexual contract underwriting the social relations of the sexes is widespread. The male sex-right undermines women's rights as free individuals. Dependency on protection for sexual favors has not been entirely removed from the reality of the marriage contract even though it is often removed from the spirit of it. Employment contracts remain institutionalized forms of control of social relations with respect to not only economic inequalities but also, and more pervasively, sexual inequalities. The 'feminization of poverty' attests to that. As women move into the labor force as independent earners, their involvement in society increases (e.g., C. Cuneo, 1990, J. Jenson, et al., 1988; H. Moroney and M. Luxton, 1987; M. Waring, 1988; and National Union of Provincial Government Employees publication, 1989). Their participation at the decision making levels, however, does not represent either their capacities or their numbers in the resource pools of available labor. The underlying assumptions which grant men authority and corresponding higher salaries remain largely in place. Those assumptions have deep roots in social patriarchy, which is inseparable from the 'God the Father' paradigm that provides a special ontological status for men. Social equality requires a vision of humanity in which women and men are self-determining persons, interacting through their mutual permeability. Goddess consciousness contributes toward that end because it allows for theory generation which is derived from lived experiences, as described in Part I.

Part III: Goddess Symbolism and Egalitarianism

In order to change the fundamental inequality between the sexes, it is useful to develop a theory of human nature which takes into account female and male sexuality that is free from the male sex-right and which is grounded in a universal creativity that may be imaged with female symbols. For that purpose, it is necessary to take femaleness as one form of normal humanity, rather than as different from the usual, normative male form. The notion of individual or person has to accommodate two sexualities. Women still have not dealt very effectively with their own sexual authority and what it means with respect to the ways in which they can know themselves and others as 'permeable selves.' Goddess consciousness includes a kind of self-consciousness where there is celebration of one's femaleness. Goddess presence within one's being is the presence of personal strength and connectedness through that strength. Autonomy and dependency are fused into a transforming process of interrelatedness. Self-determination is energized in the permeability of the self and the other. That groundedness facilitates connection with others. Self-identification through identification with Goddess power is a source of claiming the whole self. The mode of interaction is sharing. A woman who lives with a Goddess consciousness shares herself. She does not sell herself or give herself away. The alleged male sex right is no longer seen as a male birthright which underscores social organization, but rather as a convention that was historically constructed and is, therefore, open to re-interpretation. The emergence into clear view of the female birthright casts the male sex right in a different light. As women claim their birthright through connection to Goddess presence, the organizational principles governing the social relations of the sexes will become more respecting of women and, thereby, will be more empowering for men as well. Claiming their birthright as normative persons can impel women toward removing unjust social contracts and personal relations. Carol Christ helps us to do that in her various writings.

Christ emphasizes the need to affirm female sexuality in the face of the normativeness of male sexuality, both in the social and spiritual spheres. Unless the notion of 'person' can automatically assume either femaleness or maleness with the same degree of significance, there is little point in speaking of individual freedom in the abstract. Our freedom, as spiritual beings, derives from our essential natures as agents of a universal source of freedom and creativity, as described in the Introduction. Unless reference to that universal source can accommodate female and male imagery with equal force, then woman's essential self-definition as female will never be accomplished. Consequently, it is mandatory that female imagery in the name of female deity be accepted as normal. For these purposes, it is unsatisfactory merely for female imagery to be incorporated into existing male imagery or added on to it. It must be there in its own form. Female experience of spiritual creative power must be an inclusive experience of self and female-imaged creative power.

In the paradigm of 'permeable self' that I am exploring, I take sexuality to be a form of expression of spiritual energy. Of particular interest is women's sexuality because it has so often been associated with temptation or evil impulses which are in need of control (see Plaskow, 1988). In Plaskow's view, one that I support, women's sexuality is seen as positive energy that does not require the institution of marriage to control and legitimize it. It is power we are given through our connection to the eternal creative power which gives each of us the ability to live fully present to each other in those rare and wonderful moments when we are fully present to ourselves. In my view, if we are conscious of some form of eternal creative presence, then we are responsible for the exercise of it in our lives through expression of spiritual energy. If spiritual energy is intrinsic to our existence, then it is part of everyday life. In that case, it is expressed in the politics of the home, the marketplace, and in the academy where we attempt sometimes to explain the origins, nature, and destiny of humanity as though everyday activities were incidental to the project. The social relations of women and men in every sphere of human activity are affected by sexual politics. Sexual politics is about interpersonal power relations. It is about control. Women's sexuality has been controlled largely through marriage and the morality associated with that institution with regard to the respectability of women. Control of women's sexuality is so much a part of heterosexual relations that sometimes it is difficult to distinguish heterosexuality from heterosexism. Heterosexism is part of our belief in conjugal rights, namely that husbands have the right to sexual privileges with wives. Of course, wives have the same conjugal rights. But the fact that wives and husbands have the same conjugal rights does not translate into the same sense of entitlement for each of them. As we become increasingly aware of the implications of conjugal rights, martial rape becomes more of a topic for analysis and a motivation for social change.

If we view evolution as a dynamic process grounded in an eternal spiritual, creative reality and ourselves as spiritual individuals, then we, if consistent, believe that it is important to work toward a social order in which spiritual energy is expressed through individual consciousness. It is necessary, in particular, for women to experience their sexuality as positive spiritual energy. It is necessary to do so if women are to participate in the evolutionary process shaped by a theory of human nature which assumes a spiritual dimension, as does any religious interpretation of human existence. In order to live positively with our sexuality we have to experience our embodied femaleness in a strong, affirming manner. We have to reject the negativity that has been attributed to female sexuality, we have to reject our secondary sexual status. Those are initial conditions for overcoming our lack of entitlement to our own power and for beginning to respect ourselves. From that standpoint we can approach ourselves, the world, and eternal creativity on our own terms.

How do we do this with the few positive symbols, images, and concepts available to us? Do we have to rely solely on prehistoric material, which predates patriarchy? Do we have to reject all, or the majority, of the history of ideas that has come to us through the interpretations of men, shaped by their interests and wishes as embodied males? How can women begin, after so many thousands of years of relative exclusion or cooption, to speak with strength from their own points of view, as embodied females? I am fairly certain that there would be as many different responses to those questions as there are responders. I will merely attempt to give my own point of view.

The usefulness of drawing on a sexually-differentiated metaphysical creative power for self-definition is that the female person can be seen, at the ontological level, as a normal person. A group of women, then, is the equivalent of a group of persons in the same way that a group of men is. Women as female persons are to be differentiated from men as persons only according to their biology. All categories of persons, as citizens, have equal rights and responsibilities toward each other. In this view, there is neither male nor female sex-right and, accordingly, no assumed economic or marital rights over the other.

If we accept the reasonableness of female and male creative power informing us as female and male agents, then we can proceed with a discussion of 'permeable selves' as possibly mutually enlivening persons participating in egalitarian social relations. In Christ's view, when a woman experiences female creative power, she realizes herself as powerful in a way that is very improbable through experience of either a male-imaged God or as a disembodied, abstract power that does nothing to affirm her embodiedness. This is especially true in a society like ours in which women's bodies are regarded so much as commodities and objects of awareness, especially male aware-ness. Disembodied notions of creative power go part way toward affirming embodiedness, but they require imagery to flesh out personal identification with the source of one's spiritual creativity. My own experiences substantiate this claim.

Freedom of personhood requires identification of oneself with one's body.[4]   Consciousness is invariably embodied consciousness. Mary Daly points out that "as our consciousness is fragmented, we lose the thread of connectedness in our being" (1978: 386). A person is invariably embodied. A self-respecting, integrated person is one whose thread of connected-ness is in place and who claims the right of privacy as both a natural and civil right. Within the paradigm of the 'permeable self' that is being developed here, appreciation of the rights to oneself includes extension of that appreciation to the rights of others. Such a context promotes a form of sociality characterized by mutual respect of individual well-being.

The kind of individuality that is being explored here is about freedom to be individual in specifically a female or male way, without male sex-right acting as an organizing principle in social relations. If the male sex right would cease to be such a powerful and hidden factor in the social relations of the sexes, then dependency would assume a different meaning with respect to women. Sexual dependency has been closely associated with economic and intellectual dependency. If we reveal the hidden sexual contract, as Pateman does, then it is possible to dispose of it. Dependency could be better understood as the co-ordinate of self-determination (autonomy) within the paradigm of the 'permeable self.' The two modes of expression are like the convex and concave sides of a curved mirror. They are inseparable in the process of interrelated connectedness.

The notion of autonomy is problematic because of its close associations with separate, self-sufficient individualism. At the same time, I wish to preserve the power of self-determination that is given as a birthright to individuals as agents of the creative power which enables us to transcend our skin-encapsulated egos and minimizes the probability of becoming soluble selves.

As we break free of the predominant view of women as sexual beings who serve the interests of an evolutionary intentionality characterized by dominance, women are remembering how it is to experience themselves as agents. It is the remembering of something that got lost. It is like coming home to oneself, recognizing where one started out from. When a woman meets the Goddess she is obliged to live with a continued consciousness of her. That means, at least, that she must accept responsibility for the freedom she has been given. It seems that a woman who has met the Goddess must live as much as possible as an agent of the transforming power of the Goddess. To live righteously, then, is to be fully present to oneself inasmuch as one is receptive to the power of the Goddess both within one's consciousness and as one encounters it as the Other. From this perspective, living in a right relation to the Goddess is the underpinning of a right relation within the process of evolutionary transformation. Such a relation includes accepting one's sexual power and the authority it grants one to enter intersubjective relationships from the position of strength. Any theory of social evolution that takes women seriously is required to redefine women's sexuality as a positive, free expression of women's birthright.

Once we recognize the way in which the hidden sexual contract shapes the social relations between the sexes we can move on to claim our own sex-specific power. In Carol Christ's view, the most powerful way of doing that is through connections with Goddess power.

John Macquarrie (1983) writes about the metaphorical hole at the centre of our being. It is a hole filled with the spirit of God. Carol Christ would claim, and I agree with her, that for women that hole needs to be filled with Goddess spiritual power. It is the creative centre of our being where we live most importantly at home with ourselves. From there we move toward extension of ourselves, a process in which we are profoundly affected by the presence of others. Freedom to be in relation to others is coextensive with the freedom we experience in our own beings as women and men, in the presence of Goddess power or the power of God. The inclusiveness of Goddess power or the power of God reflects the inclusiveness of women and men in social relations. Righteousness is usually understood in biblical history as a right relation with God. With respect to women, it is appropriate to describe it as a right relation to the Goddess, in any of her various forms. That relation informs all social relations and mitigates oppression in its various forms. As we experience ourselves in our unique individuality, continuous with the larger creative power, we can relate in a truly human way, as female or male.

Goddess consciousness has a transformative effect on a woman with respect to her awareness of herself as both a self-determining individual and an aspect of a matrix of creative generativity. We find a means of empowerment through Goddess presence that grounds egalitarian social relations in an ontology that assumes femaleness as one of two normative modes of human existence. The two perspectives allow us to connect the spiritual, psychological, and socio-political dimensions of the 'permeable self' in personal and social evolution.

Although I am arguing for the importance of ontological claims as a platform for the evolution of social egalitarianism, it is well known that there is no necessary connection between the two. It is also generally true that dictums which refer to human equality have been more idealistic than realistic. We know that among men (i.e., males) social equality within communities of alleged free individuals is a political fiction. It has never existed in recorded history. It is, therefore, unreasonable to believe that ontological equality will establish socio-political equality between men and women. What is possible, though, is that ontological equality, based on metaphysical claims about female and male agency, would contribute toward more equitable social relations, in which sexual difference does not reflect hidden assumptions about sex-specific birthrights which shape the dominant-subordinate relations between women and men.

The paradigm of the 'permeable self,' which takes seriously the ontological claims of females and males as two normative forms of humanity, is useful not only as a contribution to social egalitarianism but it also enhances the richness of human experience. When women experience themselves as agents of a female creative power and live with their ontological creativity, it is reasonable to postulate that they may contribute

toward greater creativity through richness of difference between
themselves and men. Men would benefit from such transformative interaction, rather than being robbed of their own power
in the face of women's creativity. The process through which
such transformation might occur can be described in two steps.
First, a man who experiences a woman living from her own
strength and who affirms her in doing so is, at the same time,
affirming his own humanity as a participant in the process of
human transformation. That is one step in the interaction
between permeable selves. Second, his experience of her
experience of him as a supportive agent would likely have a
transforming effect on him. This paradigm of the 'permeable
self,' in which there is a mutual relation of enlivenment, is
contrasted sharply with the paradigm of separate and soluble
self, in which one person appropriates another, or, where power
dynamics dictate manipulative, feminine wiles be used to elicit
support from a masculinized authoritarian figure. Within the
paradigm of the 'permeable self,' ontological claims to
normativeness of femaleness and maleness provide greater
generativity in the richness of human interaction.

    We can conclude, then, that ontological normativeness
of femaleness and maleness, experienced through Goddess and
God imagery, provides a grounding for sexual equality in social
attitudes and practices.

    The God symbolism would have to be from the 'God as
Spirit' paradigm. G.W.H. Lampe (1977) says that "To speak
of 'the Spirit of God' or 'Holy Spirit' is to speak of transcendent God becoming immanent in human personality, for in his
experience of inspiration and divine indwelling man is brought
into personal communion with God's real presence" (Lampe,
1977: 61). Lampe's thesis of 'God as Spirit' is characterized
wholly by male symbolism. That is typical of traditional, male-
centered scholarship. While his approach is very useful and
inspiring, it is limited in its application to women who do not
any longer, or who never have, internalized male imagery into

their own self-definition as women. Still, there is much to be
appreciated in the paradigm of 'God as Spirit' insofar as it is
compatible with Goddess presence for women. The inter-
changeability of Goddess and God imagery in a single person's
consciousness seems altogether probable. That is an area that
requires further exploration in another paper. The task in this
paper has been to bring into focus discussion of Goddess
presence for women, which contributes toward greater transformative interaction among persons of both sexes.

Female independent sexuality, like male sexuality, is our
ontological birthright and is, therefore, the legitimate starting
point for mutually transforming, egalitarian relations between
women and men. Goddess consciousness facilitates the realization of the individual as permeable and directs sociality toward
cooperation and integration.

Notes

1. Several colleagues were helpful in the development of this
   paper. I wish especially to thank Ms. Donna Cooley
   (Jungian counsellor), Ms. Hope Olson (Librarian, Univer-
   sity of Alberta), Professor Peter Schouls (Philosophy,
   University of Alberta), Professor Karl Tomm (Psychiatry,
   University of Calgary), and Professor Petra von Morstein
   (Philosophy, University of Calgary).

2. Sally McFague's *Models of God* provides many helpful
   insights with respect to variations on the 'God the Father'
   model. This paper intends to break out of that framework
   altogether and move beyond 'God-talk' to 'Goddess-talk'.
   Whether one chooses to work continuously or discontinu-
   ously with the patriarchal model seems to be determined,
   in part at least, by how one perceives the central tenets of
   the particular tradition (Jewish, Christian, or Islamic). If

they are perceived to be not irretrievably sexist, then perhaps one remains within the traditional framework to modify it. If, on the other hand, the basic tenets are considered to be unredeemably male-centred, then one attempts to create another framework, i.e., post-patriarchal/post-traditional. This paper is an attempt to contribute to a post-traditional interpretive framework for discussion of universal creative powers experienced through female imagery.

3. See for example, Christ, *Laughter of Aphrodite*; Downing, *The Goddess;* Eisler, *The Chalice and the Blade*; Falk and Gross, *Unspoken Worlds*; Gimbutas, *The Language of the Goddess*; Markale, *Women of the Celts*; Morton, *The Journey is Home*; Plaskow and Christ, eds., *Weaving the Visions*; and Spretnak and Capra, *Green Politics*.

4. Incidentally, Locke's notion of individual requires identification with the body for his definition of individual as an owner of properties in his person or owner of anything, for that matter. An abstract, disembodied individual could not be identified as an owner of property. Indeed as Schouls points out, in his *Essays* 3.11.16, Locke says "We mean nothing by Man, but a corporeal rational Creature" (Schouls, 1980: 198, footnote 9).

References

Allen, Paula Gunn. Grandmother of the Sun. *Weaving the Visions: New Patterns in Feminist Spirituality*, Judith Plaskow and Carol P. Christ, eds. San Francisco: Harper & Row, 1989, pp. 15-21.

Belenky, Mary, et al. *Women's Ways of Knowing: The Development of Self, Voice and Mind*. New York: Basic Books, 1986.

Cuneo, Carl J. *Pay Equity: The Labour-Feminist Challenge*. Toronto: Oxford University Press, 1990.

Christ, Carol P. Rethinking Theology and Nature. *Weaving the Visions: New Patterns in Feminist Spirituality*, Judith Plaskow and Carol P. Christ, eds. San Francisco: Harper & Row, 1989, pp. 314-25.

_____. Embodied Thinking: Reflections on Feminist Theological Method. *Journal of Feminist Studies in Religion*. Vol. 5, No. 1, 1989 (Spring), 7-17.

_____. *Laughter of Aphrodite: Reflections on a Journey to the Goddess*. San Francisco: Harper & Row, 1987.

Daly, Mary. *Gyn/Ecology: The Metaethics of Radical Feminism*. Boston: Beacon Press, 1978.

Downing, Christine. *The Goddess: Mythological Images of the Feminine*. New York: Crossroads, 1984.

Eisler, Raine. *The Chalice & The Blade: Our History, Our Father*. San Francisco: Harper & Row, 1987.

Falk, Nancy and Gross, Rita. *Unspoken Worlds: Women's Religious Lives*. San Francisco: Harper & Row, 1989.

Gadon, Elinor W. *The Once & Future Goddess*. New York: Harper & Row, 1989.

Gilligan, Carol. *In a Different Voice*. Cambridge, MA: Harvard, 1982.

Gimbutas, Marija. *The Language of the Goddess*. New York: Harper & Row, 1989.

Gould, Carol C. Private Rights and Public Virtues: Women, the Family and Democracy. *Beyond Domination*, ed. Carol C. Gould. Totowa, NJ: Wowman and Allanheld, 1983.

Hill, Sharon Bishop. Autonomy and Self-Determination. *Philosophy and Women*, eds. Sharon Bishop and Marjorie Weinzweig. Belmont: Wadsworth, 1979.

Jenson, Jane; Hagen, Elizabeth; and Reddy, Ceallaigh, eds. *Feminization of the Labor Force: Paradoxes and Promises*. New York: Oxford University Press, 1988.

Keller, Catherine. *From a Broken Web: Separation, Sexism, and Self*. Boston: Beacon, 1986.

Lampe, G.W.H. *God as Spirit*. Oxford: Clarendon Press, 1977.

Lloyd, Genevieve. Feminist Philosophy and the Idea of the Feminine. Unpublished paper presented at the Annual Meeting of the Canadian Society for Women in Philosophy. Dalhousie University, Halifax, Nova Scotia, Canada, 1986.

Lorde, Audre. Uses of the Erotic. *Weaving the Visions: New Patterns in Feminist Spirituality*. Judith Plaskow and Carol P. Christ, eds. San Francisco: Harper & Row, 1989.

Luke, Helen M. *Women, Earth, and Spirit: The Feminine in Symbol and Myth*. New York: Crossroad Publishing Co., 1989.

Markale, Jean. *Women of the Celts*. Trans, A. Mygind, C. Hauch and P. Henry. Rochester, Vermont: Inner Traditions International Ltd., 1986.

Maroney, Heather Jon and Luxton, Meg. *Feminism and Political Economy: Women's Work, Women's Struggles*. Toronto: Methuen, 1987.

McFague, Sally. *Models of God: Theology for an Ecological, Nuclear Age*. Philadelphia: Fortress Press, 1987.

Morton, Nelle. *The Journey is Home*. Boston: Beacon Press, 1985.

National Union of Provincial Government Employees. *Canadian Women at Work: Their Situation, Their Union Status, and The Influence of the Public Sector: Background Paper*. Minister of Supply and Services Canada Cat. No. MP1-5-1988, 1989.

Noddings, Nel. *Caring: A Feminine Approach to Ethics and Moral Education*. Berkeley: University of California, 1984.

Macquarrie, John. *In Search of Humanity: A Theological and Philosophical Approach*. New York: Crossroad, 1983.

Pateman, Carole. *The Sexual Contract*. Standford: Standford University Press, 1988.

Plaskow, Judith and Christ, Carol P., eds. *Weaving the Visions: Patterns in Feminist Spirituality.* San Francisco: Harper & Row, 1989.

Scheman, Naomi. Individualism and the Objects of Psychology. *Discovering Reality*, Sandra Harding and Merrill B. Hintikka, eds. Boston: D. Reidel, 1983, pp. 225-44.

Schouls, Peter. *The Imposition of Method: A Study of Descartes and Locke.* Oxford: Clarendon Press, 1980.

Spretnak, Charlene and Capra, Fritjof. *Green Politics: The Global Promise.* Santa Fe: Bear Books, 1990.

Tomm, Winnifred A. Sexuality, Rationality, and Spirituality. *Zygon*, Vol. 25, No. 2, June 1990, pp. 219-37.

_____. Autonomy and Interrelatedness: Spinoza, Hume, and Vasubhandhu. *Zygon*, Vol. 22, No. 4, December 1987, pp. 459-78.

Waring, Marilyn. *If Women Counted: A New Feminist Economics.* San Francisco: Harper & Row, 1988.

Wendell, Susan. Oppression, Victimization, Choice and Responsibility. Unpublished paper, Departments of Philosophy and Women's Studies Program, Simon Fraser University, Burnaby, British Columbia, Canada, 1989.

Ywahoo, Dhynai. Renewing the Sacred Hoop. *Weaving the Visions: New Patterns in Feminist Spirituality.* Judith Plaskow and Carol P. Christ, eds. San Francisco: Harper & Row, 1989.

GODDESSES, FEMINISTS, AND SCHOLARS

Katherine K. Young

Introduction

It is often claimed that goddesses have nothing to do with women. This claim is related to the discovery that the presence of goddesses in a culture does not necessarily mean that women hold power. Indeed, there may be an inverse relation. In that case, there would be no point in beginning this journal with an issue on goddesses. If this claim is true in some contexts, though, it is not true in others. The presence of goddesses may indicate dual sex symbolism, for instance, and a social structure where women and men are viewed as different but equal. There are other kinds of relations, moreover, between goddesses and women. How we study goddesses, for example, may be informed by how we view the advancement of women in our own society.

One project of feminism is to reread history through a gynocentric lens. Some feminists view this as a necessary corrective to the androcentric lens. By recovering women as actors in history, by restoring their accomplishments whenever possible, and by documenting the subordination of women, they hope to set the record straight. But others take this a step further and argue for the need to create a feminist view of history in which women are not only agents but dominant agents. Drawing on the older theories of Bachofen, Marx, Engels, Frazer, and Briffault which contributed to the case for a matriarchal stage of history, they offer their own revision. Because anthropologists now claim that there is no evidence for matriarchy, however, these feminists prefer terms such as matristic, matrilineal, matrilocal, matrifocal and gynocentric.

Put simply, the Golden Age was a prehistoric society in which women dominated and "The Goddess" prevailed. The Fall was a male takeover, often violent, symbolized by a supreme male deity. Human society, so the reconstruction goes, moved from a time of peace to a time of war. It also moved from a time of female power to female subordination. The corollary to this view of history is that women are peaceful even when powerful, and therefore moral, while men are violent when powerful, and therefore immoral. The conclusion, of course, is that women must now restore the Golden Age by restoring "The Goddess" to her rightful place. They must also rescue people from the immoral hegemony of men. Some women are willing to rescue men as long as they can be converted and rehabilitated. Others think that men are inherently evil and so women must live separately in "womanspace." Rescuing women from the hegemony of men also involves rescuing them from the male monopoly on the interpretation of the past. This includes revising history with feminist goals in mind. In the final analysis, though, revising history really means rewriting or even remaking history.

In her book, *The Creation of Patriarchy*,[1] Gerda Lerner says that her historical reconstruction is based on the archaeological and textual record of ancient Near Eastern civilizations. She characterizes her approach as both historical and interpretative in order to make sense of the bewildering diversity of facts. She proposes a scenario that she thinks fits the data and makes sense of the changes observed. Lerner's book is accepted as historical scholarship; she is, after all, a well-established academic who has written numerous books, is "Robinson-Edwards Professor of History" at the University of Wisconson, and has been a past president of the Organization of American Historians. But Lerner herself observes that "Revolutionary ideas can be generated only when the oppressed have an alternative to the symbol and meaning systems of those who dominate them."[2] And she says that "The system of patriarchy is a historic construct; it has a beginning; it will have an end."[3] Is Lerner revising history within the constraints imposed by archaeological artifacts and ancient texts or is she remaking history by wilfully distorting or ignoring them? In short, is her scenario a scholarly interpretation of the past or the creation of a new symbol system to deconstruct the system of patriarchy?

Another academic who may blur the line between knowledge and ideology is Marija Gimbutas, professor of European archaeology at UCLA and author of more than twenty books and two hundred articles. In her recent work, *The Language of the Goddess*,[4] Gimbutas does not speak overtly of revolutionary ideas and the need to provide women with an alternative symbol and meaning system. In fact, she states with supreme self-confidence that she is "not interested in theory. The materials speak for themselves."[5] They have been welcomed by other feminist authors. Eva C. Keuls, author of *The Reign of the Phallus*, in a remark that appears on the jacket of Gimbutas' book says: "This work, the fruit of decades of research, yields insights that totally upset traditional concepts of the forces that have shaped human history.... Gimbutas is destined to go down in history as a scholar who has profoundly affected the way we think about ourselves and where we come from." Gerda Lerner, however, who knows the tests of historical scholarship, chooses to admire the work in a different way. In a remark that also appears on the jacket of Gimbutas' book, she says: "This bold and imaginative reconstruction of earliest religious symbols based on dominance of the Great Goddess offers an alternative to androcentric explanatory systems. It can never be proven, but that it *might have been is enough to challenge, inspire, and fascinate*. An important work."

While Lerner and Gimbutas base their theories on Western source material (Near Eastern and Old European[6] respectively), they imply a universal scenario.[7] The titles of both their recent books — Lerner's *The Creation of Patriarchy* and Gimbutas' *The Language of the Goddess* — lack subtitles suggesting that they are about specific regions. These authors do not look, moreover, to comparative data provided by archaeological artifacts, ancient texts and anthropological data to substantiate the implication of universality. They resort, on the contrary, to psychology (also Western based). So it is important to discover if their theories apply to other cultural areas (not to mention the larger course of human history) before any claims about the creation of patriarchy or the nature of "The Goddess" are made. In this article, then, I will examine these two works to see if there is arbitrary selection or distortion of the regional data and to see if claims can be supported by comparative studies. More specifically, I shall examine what these authors (and several others with similar perspectives) either say or imply about four common claims: (1) that worship of "The Great Goddess" was the first form of religious expression; (2) that she was a single deity with multiple forms; (3) that her power reflected the power of women in a matrilineal society; and (4) that she was displaced by a male deity in a violent conspiracy by men. I also seek to understand the relation between feminism and scholarship from the perspective of a historian of religions.

The Great Goddess as the First Form of Religious Expression

According to Lerner,

> ... in the earliest known phases of religious worship the female force was recognized as awesome, powerful, transcendent.[8]

> ... it is from the Neolithic that we derive surviv-
> ing evidence of cave paintings and sculptures
> suggesting the pervasive veneration of the
> Mother-Goddess. We can understand why men
> and women might have chosen this as their first
> form of religious expression.[9]

Lerner notes the pervasiveness of the veneration of the Mother-
Goddess in the neolithic and chalcolithic periods. There is a
profusion of archaeological finds of female figurines, usually in
a squatting position (emphasizing breasts, navel, and vulva),
throughout Old Europe and the ancient Near East from the
seventh millennium B.C.. She implies that such pervasiveness
establishes a primacy. It is curious, however, that Lerner
begins with the neolithic rather than the upper palaeolithic
period when, from about thirty-five thousand to eight thousand
years ago, representational art appeared in some areas. While
she does say that "we need to look more closely at such
societies in the Paleolithic and early Neolithic periods,"[10] she
neglects the former. But by not examining possibly relevant data
is she neglecting a fundamental task of her profession: searching
for historical antecedents? And is her choice to omit the
palaeolithic data (and yet speak of the worship of the neolithic
"Great Goddess" as the *first* form of religious expression) a
conscious tactical step in the deconstruction of patriarchy?

It is striking that a historian, of all people, buttresses her
argument with psychology rather than palaeolithic archaeology
or comparative data from contemporary hunting and gathering
societies.

> We can understand why men and women might
> have chosen this as their first form of religious
> expression by considering the psychological bond
> between mother and child. We owe our insights
> into the complexities and importance of that bond

largely to modern psychoanalytic accounts....
The life-giving mother truly had power over life
and death.   No wonder that men and women,
observing this dramatic and mysterious power of
the female, turned to the veneration of Mother-
Goddesses.[11]

For a popular audience, this is a deft move. There have been
several theories linking historical goddesses to the universal
human experience of being born of woman. Naomi Goldenberg,
for instance, establishes a linkage between Mother (in pyscho-
analysis) and Goddess (in archaeology). According to her,

Object-relations theory's intense interest in the
deep past is, in broad terms, quite similar to that
of the contemporary Goddess religions.   Both
psychoanalysis and the new thealogies involve
participants in an extensive revery on what
happened long, long ago. In psychoanalysis, an
individual's pre-verbal past is judged to be most
important.   In Goddess religion, emphasis is
placed on the collective prehistoric past.

For both philosophies a sense of connection to
the past is cultivated for the purpose of heightening involvement in the present. In the case of
Goddess religion, this focus on the past is used
to confer a sense of reality and legitimacy on
contemporary women's experience.   Recently
published books about Goddess mythology
provide women with a compendium of female
passions and sensibilities. The myths are used to
call attention to the complexity of female experience and to dignify that experience by revealing
its ancient roots. Thus, to a large degree, God-

dess religion pursues meaning in the way that
Eliade has described in his work on the myth of
the eternal return....

Even more significant than their shared reverence
for the deep past is the fact that both Goddess
thealogy and object relations theory agree on
what, or rather *who*, is the most important part
of the past. Object relations theory departs from
classical analytic theory by replacing Freud's
deep interest in the father with its own intense
preoccupation with the mother. Like the Goddess movement in religion, object relations
theory places a woman at the beginning of the
universe and thus champions a shift from an
interest in male symbols to a focus on female
ones. Both ways of thinking pose a challenge to
the importance of the father.[12]

Goldenberg observes that "thealogians" view "The Goddess" as
primordial and seek to recover "The Goddess" from the past for
therapeutic reasons. Even if constraints are imposed by the
data, therapy is more important. Thus, if "The Goddess" were
shown by historians not to be primordial, it would still be
valuable to convince people that she is primordial in order to
end tyranny. According to Goldenberg, "by stressing those
ignored or suppressed portions of collective religious history
which refer to female figures of power, Goddess thealogy chips
away at the monolith constructed by patriarchal history. *Even
if particular facts or arguments about the history of Goddess
worship are disputed, the work of writers like Merlin Stone,
Savina Teubal, Charlene Spretnak and others loosens the male
monopoly on religious power.*"[13]
    Unlike Lerner and Goldenberg, Gimbutas takes account
of some palaeolithic evidence when discussing origins.

Food gathering gave way to food producing and
hunting to a settled way of life, but there was no
corresponding major change in the structure of
symbolism, only a gradual incorporation of new
forms and the elaboration or transformation of
the old. Indeed, what is striking is not the meta-
morphosis of the symbols over the millennia but
rather the continuity from Paleolithic times on.
The major aspects of the Goddess of the Neolithic — the birth-giver, portrayed in a naturalis-
tic birth-giving pose; the fertility-giver influenc-
ing growth and multiplication, portrayed as a
pregnant nude; the life or nourishment-giver and
protectress, portrayed as a bird-woman with
breasts and protruding buttocks; and the death-
wielder as a stiff nude ("bone") — can all be
traced back to the period when the first sculptures of bone, ivory, or stone appeared, around
25,000 B.C. and their symbols — vulvas, tri-
angles, breasts, chevrons, zig-zags, meanders,
cupmarks — to an even earlier time.[14]

Gimbutas then proceeds to document her thesis with a wealth of
feminine imagery that stretches from the palaeolithic period
through the neolithic.

Even if this substantiates the fact that feminine imagery
predominated in these periods of European prehistory (and the
case seems convincing), can we assume the universality of "In
the beginning was the Goddess"? Karl J. Narr, for instance,
warns us when speaking of the palaeolithic period that

... it is not enough ... to select a few religious
phenomena from contemporary primitive
societies and apply them to the archaeological
material. Instead, it is necessary to conduct

comprehensive comparative studies in order to
obtain a sufficiently wide range of correlations
and establish a basic correspondence of meanings.[15]

In her study of 150 tribal societies entitled *Female Power and
Male Dominance: On the Origins of Sexual Inequality*,[16]
Peggy Reeves Sanday seeks to establish precisely such a
correlation. She observes, for example, that there is a correlation between gender roles and gender symbolism in creation
stories. These stories are by no means epiphenomena, for they
reflect important concepts of sacred power. Gender symbolism
in creation stories is also related to the mode of food produc-
tion. She observes that when the environment is a source of
danger in the form of large animals which are present or
hunted, the origin symbolism tends to be masculine. By
contrast, when the environment is perceived positively and large
animals are not present or hunted, then feminine origin symbolism may occur. And when there is a combination of subsistence
activities which include both hunting large animals and gathering, then there is a dual orientation which may be reflected in
couple (or dual sex) origin symbolism.[17] Sanday examines 99
societies for which information on the type of game animals
hunted is available along with an origin story. She finds that of
those societies which have feminine gender origin symbolism,
72% hunt small game or several types of game and 28% hunt
mainly large game; of those that have couple symbolism 61%
hunt small game and 39% hunt mainly large game; and of those
which have masculine gender symbolism 48% hunt small game
and 52% hunt mainly large game. She notes that in 43 of these
99 societies, large animals are the predominant type of game
hunted. In all but 5 of these 43 societies, couple or masculine
origin symbolism is present.[18] This implies that 56 societies
in her sample hunt small game, fish, and gather plants or have
a combination of hunting large game and gathering. She does

not tell us, however, what percentage of societies have which kind of subsistence activity. Nevertheless, from this discussion we can surmise that if there is feminine symbolism in the society and there is fishing, gathering and hunting, it is more likely that the animals hunted are small game and that fishing or gathering is more important. If couple (or dual sex) symbolism is found, then it is likely that there is a combination of hunting large game and gathering or a combination of hunting small animals, fishing, and gathering, with hunting especially important.

Now, if the kind of correlations found in hunting and gathering societies are clues to the kind found in prehistoric societies — and we have no reason to reject the possibility outright since hunting was common to the latter — then we should examine what kind of hunting was done in Old Europe.

According to Gimbutas, subsistence in the palaeolithic period of Old Europe was based on hunting small animals, fishing, and gathering plants. Waterfowl was an important food supply.[19] "Geese, cranes, and swans [were] ... encountered painted or engraved on bone objects marked with chevrons and parallel lines, or as ivory figurines.... Some representations of waterbirds [were] ... clearly anthropomorphized."[20] Gimbutas argues, in fact, that the Bird Goddess was one of the earliest forms of "The Goddess" and continued into the neolithic period. Fishing was also an important subsistence activity: the fish was "associated very early with the vulva, uterus, net, zig-zag, spiral, parallel lines, and plant shoots, as can be seen on these engravings on bone or antler from Upper Paleolithic Magdalenian sites in southern France and northern Spain."[21] In neolithic art, the fish was often placed within the Goddess' womb or anthropomorphized as a goddess.[22]

Does the data furnished by Gimbutas fit Sanday's pattern observed in a large sample of hunting and gathering societies? If the dominant form of origin symbolism is feminine, as Gimbutas claims, then this would correlate with the fact that the economy consists of hunting small animals, fishing, and gathering. But is such an economy found throughout Europe at that time?

In parts of Europe in the palaeolithic period, large animals such as bison or deer were also hunted. We are reminded of Sanday's observation that when large game animals are hunted or when they are perceived as dangerous, the religious symbolism is likely to be male or dual sex. It should come as no surprise to find that horn symbolism stems from the palaeolithic period and that large antlers may represent maleness itself or men's association with large animals. We also find some male figures from the areas that hunt large animals. Gimbutas herself describes, for instance, male figures from the upper palaeolithic period and suggests that they may represent a Master of Animals:

> Horned, nude, and usually ithyphallic figures occur in Final Perigordian, Middle and Final Magdalenian, and Epipaleolithic cave engravings and paintings of France and Spain.... The most interesting and well known in archeological literature are two bison-men and the so-called "sorcerer" with stag antlers from the cave of Les Trois Freres (Ariege), France. One ... has a bison's head with large horns and a hairy pelt with a tail. He has human legs and animal arms; he is walking or dancing in an upright position.... One of the clues to the symbolic meaning of the bison-man... is his association with the animal herd. Was the bison-man a Master of Animals, a divine figure well known among the hunting peoples in the Americas and northern Eurasia? The wide distribution of a mythical figure with similar features suggests its prehistoric roots. Among the American Indians the

> Master of Animals is one of the most distinctive
> mythic ideas. He is a supernatural ruler whose
> function is to exercise stewardship over the wild
> animals, especially the animals hunted by
> men.[23]

From this palaeolithic evidence provided by Gimbutas, we
conclude that subsistence activities were different in various
parts of Europe and that religious symbolism was also somewhat
different. While the area termed Old Europe by Gimbutas had
a predominance of feminine symbolism, areas of Western
Europe which hunted large animals may have had more male or
dual sex symbolism. Thus, it cannot be argued that a goddess
is "the earliest known phase of religious worship" or the
"primordial form as the source of all." Moreover, if the
evidence varies even within Europe, it cannot be argued that the
"Great Goddess" is universally an aspect of the palaeolithic
period.

Lerner also bypasses information in her own discussion
which challenges the notion of the primordial "Great Goddess."
When speaking of a site called Çatal Hüyük, she says that

> In the lower layers of the excavation there are no
> figurative representations of humans, only bulls
> and rams, animal paintings and bull horns. Mel-
> laart interprets these as symbolic representations
> of male gods. In the 6200 B.C. layer the first
> representations of female figures appear....
> There is also one remarkable statue of a male
> and female figure embracing and next to it
> another one of a woman holding a child.[24]

If male deities or male symbols predate female figures, at least
at this site, how can Lerner speak so confidently about a
primordial "Great Goddess?"

In any case, we have found several discrepancies between the data and the interpretations. We also have found that the comparative analysis has been systematically ignored. In an age of mature scholarship and on such an important topic, it is curious that we must ponder the motives of well-known scholars in the field when they claim that "The Goddess" is primordial.

"The Great Goddess" and Monotheism

It is striking that Lerner chooses to speak of *Goddess Religion* as if it were monotheistic: there was a supreme deity (albeit with multiple forms). According to Lerner, "The Goddess"

> ... is shown amidst pillars or trees, accompanied by goats, snakes, birds. Eggs and symbols of vegetation are associated with her. These symbols indicate that she was worshipped as a source of fertility for vegetation, animals, and humans. She is represented by the Minoan snake-goddess, with her breasts exposed. She was venerated in Sumer as Ninhursag and Inanna; in Babylon as Kubab and Ishtar; in Phoenicia as Astarte; in Canaan as Anath; in Greece, as Hekate-Artemis. Her frequent association with the moon symbolized her mystical powers over nature and the seasons. The belief system manifested in Great Goddess worship was monistic and animistic. There was *unity* among earth and the stars, humans and nature, birth and death, *all of which were embodied in the Great Goddess.*

The cults of the Great Goddess were based on
the belief that it is she, in one or another of her
manifestations, who creates life. But she was
also associated with death. She was praised and
celebrated for her virginity and her maternal
qualities.... Female sexuality was sacred to her
service and honoured in her rituals.... The
duality of the Goddess represented the duality
observable in nature — night and day, birth and
death, light and darkness. Thus, in the earliest
known phases of religious worship the female
force was recognized as awesome, powerful,
transcendent.[25]

Is Lerner anachronistic? She mentions goddesses from later
Near Eastern states — Sumer, Babylon, Phonecia, Canaan,
Greece, and so forth — yet implies that she is still discussing
the pre-state neolithic "Great Goddess." Furthermore, she
herself mentions that goddesses generally became daughters and
wives of supreme gods or were relegated to various cults after
the rise of states. Whence the "awesome, powerful, transcendent" nature of "The Great Goddess?"
    Many feminists justify such ahistoric treatment when it
comes to the subject of ancient goddesses. In *The Woman's
Encyclopedia of Myths and Secrets*, for instance, Barbara G.
Walker says:

Few words are so revealing of western sexual
prejudice as the word Goddess, in contrast to the
word God. Modern connotations vastly differ
from those of the ancients to whom the Goddess
was a full-fledged cosmic parent figure who
created the universe and its laws, ruler of
Nature, Fate, Time, Eternity, Truth, Wisdom,
Justice, Love, Birth, Death, etc.

> Male writers through the centuries broke the
> Goddess figure down into innumerable "god-
> desses," using different titles or names she
> received from different peoples at different
> times. If such a system had been applied to the
> usual concept of God, there would now be a
> multitude of separate "gods" with names like
> Almighty, Yahweh, Lord, Holy Ghost, Sun of
> Righteousness, Christ, Creator, Lawgiver, Jeho-
> vah, Providence, Allah, Savior, Redeemer ... ad
> infinitum, each one assigned a particular function
> in the world pantheon.... [The] names and titles
> of the Goddess were ever more minutely clas-
> sified, and some were even masculinized, huma-
> nized, or diabolized.   Yet such classification
> tends to disintegrate under deeper study that
> reveals the same archetypal characteristics in
> nearly all the "goddesses."[26]

It is true that there were supreme male deities who incorporated
the names and epithets of many others to express the idea of
totality and supremacy. Even though such gods were associated
with cosmic symbolism, however, they were primarily associated with particular territories and nations. The historian of
religions today certainly would not subsume the supreme male
deities of different states as individual forms of the *Great God*
who is "awesome, powerful and transcendent" (to use Lerner's
terms); in that case Yahweh, Ahura Mazda, and Śiva would be
but manifestations of the one God.

   As historians of religions, moreover, can we assume that
these goddesses are different forms of one deity? According to
Gimbutas, symbols represent the

> ... grammar and syntax of a kind of metalang-
> uage by which an entire constellation of mean-

> ings is transmitted. They reveal the basic world-
> view of Old European (pre-Indo-European)
> culture ... patterns that cross the boundaries of
> time and space ... [and] indicate the extension of
> the *same* Goddess religion to all of these regions
> as a cohesive and persistent ideological sys-
> tem.[27]

If goddesses and abstract symbols are only morphologically related, they are not necessarily aspects of one deity. We can also account for similarities through diffusion. The meanings ascribed to a symbol may sometimes differ. Then, too, the same form may have a different function. Sometimes new forms are created by similar associations or similar shapes. And there may also be discontinuities. Gimbutas herself divides Old Europe into a number of different cultural zones. If everything were uniform and "monistic," why study different areas? Because we are dealing with prehistory and therefore have no textual records of how goddess images were understood at the time, we always risk ascribing (not to mention prescribing) meanings. I am sympathetic to Gimbutas who must try to interpret the enigmatic nature of neolithic symbols when there are no written records. This is not an easy task. In lieu of other evidence, it is necessary to look for clues in related cultural zones and from earlier or later periods. At the same time, it is extremely important to compare the analysis with other cross-cultural studies.

     Did people within the different cultural zones of Old Europe themselves have the idea of one great being with many manifestations or epiphanies? More importantly, was the idea of one supreme being with many manifestations known to societies before the process of state formation? Gimbutas herself is quick to point out that we moderns should not superimpose the category of Fertility Goddess or Mother Goddess on the Old European data.[28] But what about the term

"Great"?   It can be argued, in fact, that Gimbutas anachronistically superimposes it on various female figures. She refers, for example, to "the absolute rule" of the "Great Goddess" and says that "These life-givers and death-wielders are 'queens' and as such they remained in individual creeds for a very long time in spite of their official dethronement."[29]

> A remnant in the historical era of the goddesses' ruling power is indicated by the usage of the term *queen* for those who were not married to Indo-European deities but who continued to be powerful in their own right. Herodotus wrote of 'Queen Artemis' and Hesychius called Aphrodite 'the queen.' Diana, the Roman counterpart of the virgin Artemis, was invoked as *regina*.... The most inspired account in all ancient literature is contained in Lucius Apuleius' 2nd century A.D. *Golden Ass,* the earliest Latin novel, where Lucius invokes Isis from the depths of his misery. Then she appears and utters: "I am she that is the natural mother of all things, mistress and governess of all the elements, the initial progeny of worlds, chief of the powers divine, *queen of all* that are in Hell, the principal of them all that dwell in Heaven, manifested alone and under one form of all the gods and goddesses. At my will the planets of the sky, the wholesome winds of the seas, and the lamentable silences of hell be disposed; my name, my divinity is adored throughout the world, in diverse manners, in variable customs, and by many names." This text is an illumination with very precious details on the worship of the Goddess nearly 2,000 years ago.[30]

When Gimbutas says that the image of "The Goddess" as queen is a remnant in the historical era, she implies that the notion of "The Goddess" as queen is prehistoric. The language of absolute rule, queen, and dethronement, however, belongs to vocabulary that developed after the rise of states. Old Europe in the neolithic period had settlements, to be sure, but was not politically organized into states with absolute rulers.

It may be argued, moreover, that the concept of one supreme deity with multiple names, forms, and functions is a kind of monotheism which is itself a product of state formation. One of the agendas of state formation, after all, is the process of unification. If multiple deities are present and represent various interest groups in the society, then one deity which absorbs the previous ones in some way would help unite the people within a new political entity no longer based on kinship. The Hindu supreme deity Viṣṇu, for instance, has a thousand names, is creator, preserver, and destroyer of the universe, and has different incarnations (some of which were once separate figures such as Kṛṣṇa Rāma, and Buddha). More importantly, Viṣṇu's rise to the status of supreme deity paralleled the process of primary and secondary state formation in India.[31] Such a transcendent and omnipotent deity also parallels the imagery of the divine, all-powerful human ruler.

If supreme deities with multiple forms and images such as queens arise with state formation, it is highly questionable to subsume all explicitly female figures (or symbols associated with them) under the concept of "one deity," much less a "Great Deity" (in the sense of a supreme being who has absolute power) or a "queen" in the neolithic period. In the neolithic context, on the contrary, it is more likely that female figures were not viewed as "supreme" but rather as immanent powers which articulated the human concern with the regeneration of life. (Another possibility is that each female deity was viewed, in turn, as most important among many — a phenomenon in Vedic India, which has been termed henotheism by Max

Müller).   It is obvious, then, why Gimbutas must turn to Herodotus and Hesychius (who wrote after the formation of states in Greece) and to a Latin work from the height of the Roman Empire to find goddesses who are queens and supreme deities. Gimbutas may also have been influenced by the contemporary movement for women's "empowerment." The desire to see women in positions of power or images of powerful goddesses as role models may, consciously or unconsciously, be a reason for the anachronism of imputing power to palaeolithic or neolithic figures and making them into divine queens with absolute power. This takes us to the next point.

Like male priests in monotheistic religions, Gimbutas refuses to recognize any other deity. Accordingly, she has to ignore or explain away the evidence of male or dual sex symbolism, which is illustrated in her own book in order to maintain the view that "The Great Goddess" is "parthenogenic." Gimbutas begins her section on male images with a quote from William Irwin Thompson. "The natural rhythm of the male is a phallic one of rise and fall.... The myths would, therefore, quite naturally tell stories in which the male is the climactic, tragic figure of flourish and vanish."[32] This may provide the reason for her subsequent statement: "Phallic cult articles ... do not represent a male god but rather a vivifying and fructifying force of nature appearing as an aspect of life column symbolism; or they are fused with the divine feminine body and subsumed to the power of the Goddess."[33]

> The phallus is often used with the female body, whose inherent power is enhanced by the life force manifested in the column. On this Upper Paleolithic figurine of stealite (or serpentine marble), the head is replaced by a featureless phallus.... The Old European phallus is far from being the obscene symbol of our days. Rather, it is close to what is still found in India, the

lingam a sacred cosmic pillar inherited from the Neolithic Indus valley civilization.... One of the earliest such representations in Europe is a fusion of the phallus with the divine body of the God- dess, which begins in the Upper Paleolithic. Some of the "Venuses" of this period have phallic heads with no facial features.... The same phenomenon is encountered in southeastern Europe during the Neolithic until about 5000 B.C..... Among the Starcevo figurines of the mid-6th millennium B.C. are some whose form is that of male genitals; the upper part is phallic and the lower buttocks are shaped like tes- ticles.[34]

It is striking that Gimbutas says: "This female figurine has a phallic head whose lower part may be shaped like testicles."[35] Later she elaborates:

Although the male element is attached, these figurines remain essentially female. They do not represent a fusion of two sexes but rather an enhancement of the female with the mysterious life force inherent in the phallus. The Goddess figurine creates a base from which the phallus, understood as a cosmic pillar, rises. It comes from her womb in the same way that stalagmites and stalactites grow from her womb in the cave.[36]

This discussion is filled with contradictions. On the one hand, Gimbutas suggests that the female aspect of these figures is somehow more basic than the male. But elsewhere she writes that from "the bucranium or body of the sacrificed bull, new life emerges in an epiphany of the Goddess as flower, tree, column of watery substance, bee, or butterfly."[37] She interprets the phallic element as the pillar of life and suggests that it has nothing to do with the male organ. At the same time, she herself gives examples in which the shape of the penis and testicles is obvious. One example is particularly striking. She describes a figure — she calls it a female figure — having a high cylindrical neck with a "mushroom" head and no facial features. "When viewing the object from the back," she notes, "we see an anatomically correct rendition of the male genitalia, an erect penis and scrotum with the genital ridge represented by a deep groove.... When viewed from top and bottom ... however, the sculpture resembles female genitalia."[38] It is strange that she calls this particular sculpture a female figure yet marvels at its perfect dual sex imagery. It is also strange that she suggests that such a figure is not "the obscene symbol;" rather, it is the cosmic pillar. Such examples, on the contrary, establish beyond a doubt that phallic imagery is commonplace. While the *lingam* in India is considered a cosmic pillar, it is also a form of the male supreme god Śiva. And despite the reluctance of modern Hindus to view the *lingam* as the male organ, this equation is well established in many sculptures and texts.

Does Gimbutas have a non-scholarly agenda when she interprets her data to prove that "The Great Goddess" is singular and supreme? It is one thing to argue that female symbolism is dominant in Old Europe. It is quite another, however, to suggest that it alone exists, that it is always central, or that "divine bisexuality ... stresses *her* absolute power."[39] By observing that the male is attached but not essential, or that the male force enhances the female but does not fuse with it, Gimbutas is overinterpreting the evidence. From the discussion of Sanday in the previous section, we recall that dual sex symbolism may also exist in societies where small game animals are hunted and is common where there is a combination of large game hunting and gathering.

Gimbutas herself provides ample evidence of this. Nude women hold bison horns; bison heads are associated with plants, seeds, and nuts; bison horns are depicted as moon crescents; and so forth. Bison and their horns, as mentioned previously, were likely a male symbol or symbolized male interests (hunting large animals) in certain parts of Europe. If plants, seeds, and moon crescents are feminine symbols or symbolize feminine interests, then the above pairing would represent dual sex symbolism. Even here, however, Gimbutas undermines the dual sex symbolism by describing a painting of a bison which appears on the main panel in the centre of a cave in the following manner: "Its central position probably derives from the intimate relationship between the bison and the Goddess; the fact that the woman and the bison both have a pregnancy of nine months may help account for this connection."[40] (But, of course, the bison is the animal hunted and the horns may symbolize the male principle). "With the advent of sedentary life," she goes on to observe, "horns, bucrania, bull figurines, and tauromorphic vases become omnipresent in the art of the Near East and Old Europe."[41]

Instead of admitting that dual sex symbolism seems to increase over time, Gimbutas suggests that the head of the bull is prominent because of "the extraordinary likeness of the female uterus and fallopian tubes to the head and horns of a bull."[42] She refers to an explanation given by Dorothy Cameron in her book *Symbols of Birth and Death in the Neolithic Era*. Cameron says that people would have noticed the shape of the fallopian tubes when birds of prey eat the flesh of the exposed body after death. Because the body is laid flat, moreover, the fallopian tubes which are normally turned downward would be turned upwards. This would resemble the head of the bull with its upward turned horns. Gimbutas concludes: "In the end, it has become clear that the prominence of the bull in this symbolic system comes not from that animal's strength and muscularity, as in Indo-European symbolism, but rather from the accidental similarity between its head and the female reproductive organs."[43]   This explanation appears extremely farfetched, especially when there is other evidence for dual sex symbolism. It is highly doubtful that anyone would have observed the miniscule fallopian tubes. And it is even more doubtful that vultures would eat just the right amount to expose the fallopian tubes and uterus so that someone could see them all together. Finally, it is extremely doubtful that anyone would have known that these tubes were connected with reproduction since the human egg itself was only discovered in modern times.[44]

One wonders how Gimbutas can speak of a supreme, *parthenogenic creator*, who creates from her own substance, when symbols of male and female organs so often appear together. She assumes that there was no awareness that males are necessary for reproduction. On the contrary, most societies studied by anthropologists speak of sperm or intercourse as a necessary if not sufficient condition for pregnancy.[45] According-ing to Gimbutas, the fact that there is no evidence of a marriage between the Earth Mother and the Sky Father suggests the parthenogenic nature of "The Great Goddess." But the subsis-tence of Old Europe being based on hunting small game animals, fishing, and agriculture would have a different type of symbolism, one that is more immanent. This does not rule out the possibility of some dual sex imagery. Such imagery, furthermore, need not be anthropomorphic.

A connection has been made between the omnipotence of "The Goddess" and the power of women in neolithic societies. It has been claimed that women, as mothers, had sole power over life and death in prehistoric times. But did they? Some feminists today suggest that men have always been useless. Nevertheless, men have been necessary for the renewal of the species and have made fundamental contributions to the group by protecting it and by providing food (animal protein) and other products from game animals. The size, strength, and mobility of men (not to mention their genetic contribution to reproduction) must have had evolutionary importance. Otherwise, human reproduction would have been asexual (through parthenogenesis).

Lerner correctly challenges the simplistic view of biological determinism, that men's "greater physical strength, their ability to run faster and lift heavier weights, and their greater aggressiveness"[46] give them categorical supremacy. She notes that these biological qualities contributed to gender roles based on what was functional and ensured the survival of the species in early times. I have no quarrel with this view, but I find it curious that she, having made this observation, systematically downplays the male contribution elsewhere in her discussion. Even while speaking of complementarity, she speaks of mother and child as the *most basic dyad*. But the idea of the mother-child dyad neglects how fathers also bond to their biological or social children and is contrary to evidence of the pair-bonding of men and women, which is thought to have existed already among earlier hominids such as *homo erectus* or *homo habilis*.[47] Lerner suggests, moreover, that the "infant's survival *depended* on the quality of maternal care."[48] According to her, "the first sexual division of labor, by which men did the big-game hunting and children and women ... food gathering, seems to derive from biological sex differences. These biological sex differences are not differences in the size and endurance of men and women but solely reproductive differences, specifically women's ability to nurse babies."[49] She also writes that "The ego formation of the individual male, which must have taken place within a context of fear, awe, and possibly dread of the female, must have led men to create social institutions to bolster their egos, strengthen their self-confidence, and validate their sense of worth."[50] Such statements suggest the biological redundancy of men and ignore the fact that biological fathers (or the men of the group) also contributed to infant survival through providing food, protection, and so forth. The quality of male care certainly was not incidental to survival in those times. If hunting and gathering societies were egalitarian, as the evidence suggests, then it is hard to believe that there was such a male identity crisis. The comparative advantages of male size, strength and mobility along with the esteem derived from their efforts at hunting may have contributed in no small measure to healthy male ego formation at that time.

Be that as it may, it is now common in some feminist circles to argue that it is necessary for women to withdraw into "womanspace." There is no need for men, they believe, in the lives of women and children. Is it a coincidence that just at the moment when women are fighting for reproductive autonomy — and when human parthenogenesis is technologically possible[51] — that discussions of the "redundant male" occur on television talk shows and in books,[52] that theories of the primacy and parthenogenic nature of "The Great Goddess" become popular, and that history is "interpreted" in this light?

"The Great Goddess" in a Matrilineal Society

With the domestication of plants, says Lerner, women's importance in subsistence activities increases. Horticultural society, according to Lerner, is a period "when matrilineal, matrilocal systems abound ... [and] group survival demands the demographic equalization of men and women."[53] Now, this statement is curious: if hunting and gathering societies are relatively egalitarian, why the demand for demographic equalization of men and women? And if matrilineal societies exist and imply the dominance of women, why speak of the need for equalization in the first place?

Gimbutas also assumes that the societies of Old Europe are matrilineal. Like Lerner, she pays lip service in her introduction to the idea of social egalitarianism: "A balanced, nonpatriarchal and nonmatriarchal social system is reflected by religion, mythologies, and folklore, by studies of the social structure of Old European and Minoan cultures."[54] She offers no documentation from the neolithic period, however, to indicate what society was like. It is striking that this sentence is immediately preceded by one suggesting matriarchy: "The Goddess-centered art with its striking absence of images of warfare and male domination, reflects a social order in which women *as heads of clans or queen-priestesses* played a central part."[55] We have already reviewed the problem of queens in neolithic societies prior to state formation.

But there is another problem with her discussion. Even if we were to accept for the moment that Old Europe and the ancient Near East were matrilineal (and this may have been generally the case in these regions), can we build a larger theory on this data? Are neolithic societies *always* matrilineal? In his foreward to *The Language of the Goddess*, Joseph Campbell supports the view that neolithic societies were matrilineal (if not matriarchal).

In the library of European scholarship the first recognition of such a matristic order of thought and life antecedent to and underlying the historical forms of both Europe and the Near East appeared in 1861 in Johann Jakob Bachofen's *Das Mutterrecht*, where it was shown that in the codes of Roman Law vestigial features can be recognized of a matrilineal order of inheritance. Ten years earlier, in America, Lewis H. Morgan had published in *The League of the Ho-de-no-sau-nee, or Iroquois*, a two-volume report of a society in which such a principle of "Mother Right" was still recognized; and in a systematic review, subsequently, of kinship systems throughout America and Asia, he had demonstrated *an*

all but worldwide distribution of such a prepatri-
archal order of communal life.   Bachofen's
recognition, around 1871, of the relevance of
Morgan's work to his own marked a break-
through from an exclusively European to a
planetary understanding of this sociological
phenomenon. There is to be recognized in Marija
Gimbutas's reconstruction of the "Language of
the Goddess" a far broader range of historical
significance, therefore, than that merely of Old
Europe, from the Atlantic to the Dnieper, c.
7000-3500 B.C.[56]

While Lerner rules out matriarchy, she gives great
importance to the evidence for matrilineal societies in the
neolithic age and the fact that they disappear with the gradual
change to state formation. We have already noted her claim
that in horticultural societies, matrilineal, matrilocal systems
abound. Despite her many caveats and rehearsals of multiple
causes (which we cannot go into here), she emphasizes one
argument, which becomes the crux of her theory. She says that
"the kinship *shift from matriliny to patriliny must be a significant turning point in the relation of the sexes, and must be
coincident with the subordination of women.*"[57] And she says
that "approximately at the time when hunting/gathering or
horticulture gives way to agriculture, kinship arrangements *shift
from matriliny to patriliny and private property develops.*"[58]
All this implies that a stage of matrilineality is common and can
be viewed as the norm prior to the birth of patriarchy. Moreover, as we have noted earlier, there is always the inuendo that
this scenario is not just peculiar to the ancient Near East but a
more general theory for the birth of patriarchy. It is curious
that Lerner herself also offers evidence that is contrary to such
a reconstruction yet fails to notice the discrepancy:

> It is in horticultural societies that we most fre-
> quently find women dominant or highly influen-
> tial in the economic sphere. In a sample survey
> of 515 horticultural societies, women dominate
> cultivation activities in 41 percent of the cases ...
> In the horticultural societies studied, most are
> patrilineal, despite women's decisive economic
> role.[59]

Just as a majority of horticultural societies in the anthropological
record have been patrilineal (or bilateral), it is likely that many
neolithic societies would also have been *patrilineal*. Accordingly, if neolithic societies of Old Europe and the ancient Near
East were matrilineal, it is a regional phenomenon at best.
Since many neolithic societies in other cultural zones have been
patrilineal (or bilateral), moreover, it is problematic to recon-
struct a global evolutionary model on Old European and Near
Eastern evidence. Sanday, for instance, cites findings of
Murdock and Wilson that "In the total Standard Cross-Cultural
Sample of 186 societies, 26 (14%) are classified in the
matrilineal descent category and 38 (21%) follow the matrilocal
rule of residence."[60]

Lerner states that "we can assert that female subordination is not universal, even though we have no proof for the
existence of a matriarchal society. But women, like men, have
a deep need for a coherent system of explanation that not only
tells us what is and why it got to be as it is but allows for an
alternate vision of the future."[61] Once again, is there an
ideological agenda behind her assumption of matrilineality?

The fact that there is at least nominal male dominance in
matrilineal societies is rarely addressed by feminists who use the
matrilineal data. Because they prefer to view the power of
women as an expression of independence, they rarely speak of
neolithic women in the context of bonding with men (brother or
husband) just as they prefer to speak of "The Great Goddess"

as independent. It is to Lerner's credit that she does observe that "In most matrilineal societies, it is a male relative, usually the woman's brother or uncle *who controls* economic and family decisions."[62] And yet her assumption, when constructing her explanatory theory, is that matrilineality reflects the power of women. It is true, of course, that in matrilineal societies women have some real power because the lineage passes through their line. If the subsistence of the matrilineal society is also based primarily on horticulture, women may have power over the food supply as well. Thus, the positive correlation between women's economic participation and status is important for anyone contemplating how contemporary societies should be changed. To ignore the mechanism by which women and men bond for clan or family stability, as is common in many discussions today, is, however, historically unprecedented and points to a radically new view, that of two separate societies, one of men and one of women and children.

This discussion is particularly important in light of the fact that matrilineal societies seemed to have posed particular problems for men. According to David M. Schneider and Kathleen Gough, the conflict between a man's position as brother in the matriclan and as biological father has been termed the "matrilineal puzzle."[63] A.R. Radcliffe-Brown and Daryll Forde speak of the tensions inherent in this social structure:

> ... the ways in which domestic authority is divided between a man and the head of his wife's kinship group are surprisingly varied. In some cases there is a formal allocation of rights and privileges between father and mother's brother in return for service and payments. In other cases the balance is less well defined, and every marriage produces what can only be described as a constant pull-father-pull-mother's brother, in which the personality, wealth, and social status

of the two individuals or their respective kinsmen
give the advantage to one side or the other....

... the dominant principle of Ashanti kinship is
the rule of matrilineal descent.... The chief
problem of kinship relations among them is to
adjust the jural and moral claims and bonds
arising out of marriage and fatherhood to those
imposed by matrilineal kinship.   Conflict
between these rival claims and bonds is inherent
in their kinship system.[64]

There were other problems that men faced besides conflicting
kinship ties and the dilemma of loyalty. The anthropological
record shows that the biological father was often marginalized:

In matrilineal descent groups the emotional
interest of the father in his own children constitutes a source of strain....[65]

In other words, while in matriliny different
fathers do not necessarily matter or are incidental, in patriliny mothers always matter, even if
only as indices of discreteness....[66]

Many men also complain bitterly that they and
their kin are forgotten by their sons and daughters, who are said to remember only their mother's people.[67]

If matrilineality posed a problem for men, then there are
reasons why men may have preferred a patrilineal system. It
was not simply a desire to subjugate women as has often been
claimed.

There is one last assumption about "the Great Goddess" in a matrilineal society. It is the assumption that such societies are peaceful. It is well established, however, that there was violence associated with sacrifice. Gimbutas herself furnishes us evidence for this:

> Womblike caves ... were sanctuaries. At Scaloria in ... southeastern Italy ... one hundred and thirty-seven skeletons, most of which were in a mass burial and had traces of peculiar cuts at the base of their skulls, were found.... Perhaps Death and Regeneration Mysteries were celebrated here.... In the analagous [sic] vagina-uterus-shaped cave of Koutala on the Cycladaic island of Serifos ... a stalagmite appears in the form of a female figure. In front of it were the remains of offerings — Neolithic dishes, animal bones, and charred material.[68]

Moreover, there have also been matrilineal societies which have practiced raiding or warfare (such as the Bedouin of pre-Islamic Arabia and the Nayar of Kerala). In fact, conflict between groups is probably as old as early hominids. Groups no doubt protected their own hunting territory and fought intruders. They also may have tried to take territory from others, especially if animals had become scarce or if there were drought.[69] The issue of war takes us to the next section.

The Fall: the Male Takeover and the Beginning of Evil

Lerner describes the Fall of "The Goddess" as follows:

> Sometime during the agricultural revolution relatively egalitarian societies with a sexual

division of labor based on biological necessity
gave way to more highly structured societies in
which both private property and the exchange of
women based on incest taboos and exogamy were
common.   The earlier societies were often
matrilineal and matrilocal, while the later surviv-
ing societies were predominantly patrilineal and
patrilocal.   Nowhere is there any evidence of a
reverse   process,   going   from   patriliny   to
matriliny. The more complex societies featured
a division of labor no longer based only on
biological distinctions, but also on hierarchy and
the power of some men over other men and all
women. A number of scholars have concluded
that the shift here described coincides with the
formation of the archaic state. It is with this
period then that theoretical speculation must end,
and historical inquiry begin.[70]

My thesis is that, just as the development of
plow agriculture, coinciding with increasing
militarism, brought major changes in kinship and
in gender relations, so did the development of
strong kingships and of archaic states bring
changes in religious beliefs and symbols. The
observable pattern is: first, the demotion of the
Mother Goddess figure and the ascendance and
later dominance of her male consort/son; then his
merging with a storm-god into a male Creator-
God, who heads the pantheon of gods and goddesses. Wherever such changes occur, the power
of creation and of fertility is transferred from the
Goddess to the God ... [These changes are
accompanied by changes in symbols] from (1)
the vulva of the goddess to the seed of man; (2)

from the tree of life to the tree of knowledge; (3)
from the celebration of the Sacred Marriage to
the Biblical covenants.[71]

Lerner notes that the concept of creation changes over time
from being "merely the acting out of the mystic force of female
fertility to being a conscious act of creation, often involving
god-figures of both sexes"[72] such as a son or brother who
mates with the Mother Goddess, and who may have to die
before he can be reborn. With the development of writing and
the elaboration of various symbol systems, come several
changes: the symbolization of the capacity to create; an erosion
of the Mother Goddess as the sole principle of creativity; and an
increase in the importance of masculine imagery beginning with
the gods of wind, air or thunder, who come to reflect the
earthly king. These changes, argues Lerner, may be correlated
with the rise of archaic states (beginning in the third millennium
B.C.) which emphasized male kingship and military leadership.
This process is completed by the rise of two national gods,
Marduk and Ashur, to supreme power parallel to the development of two rival national states headed by absolute monarchs.
Similarly, Baal, a young storm God, becomes head of the
pantheon in Canaanite mythology while Anath, once a fierce
warrior and the granter of fertility, is overshadowed.   A
corollary of this change is that the Mother-Goddess appears as
the wife or daughter of a vegetation-god. She also proliferates
into a variety of forms which remain vital in popular religion.
Her powers are transferred to males. Male priests, for instance,
become increasingly influential at the centre of the nation and
its national mythology.

     Once again, though, is this scenario confined to the Near
East or are there other examples of the so-called "patriarchal
revolution"? It is certainly true that there are other examples of
this phenomenon in the history of religions. One could argue,
for instance, that the Chinese penchant for female symbolism

(especially in philosophical Taoism with its concept of the Valley or Mother of the World and popular Taoism with figures such as the Great Goddess of the West) is a clue to the possibility that goddesses were important in the neolithic period.[73] With the development of the Shang Dynasty and the formation of the archaic state, however, goddesses would have been replaced or marginalized by the supreme god Shang Ti in the image of an omnipotent king (though they may have made a comeback later in history at a time when the empire was stabilized). Whatever the earliest social structure (and some have argued that it was matrilineal),[74] the social organization became patrilineal. There is the possibility, of course, that dual sex symbolism was also present because neolithic subsistence activities included raising animals (pigs, sheep, oxen) and agriculture (millet, wheat, barley). (Sanday suggests that a dual economy consisting of animal husbandry and agriculture may be reflected in dual sex symbolism.[75]) Representing the cooperation of male and female (and a unity which embraces duality), the *yin/yang* symbol of later times in China may reflect the idea that both men and women had once contributed fundamentally to the food supply.

Similarly, Robert S. Ellwood has provided plausible arguments from clues in the *Nihonshoki Sujin Chronicle*,[76] for a "patriarchal revolution" in ancient Japan in the 4th century C.E. — just when a nation was developing out of the neolithic villages. The first period witnessed a "horizontal cosmology;" the sea and the female goddess Amaterasu (possessor of the empress Jingo) were important. With the rise of the Sujin dynasty (which may or may not have been related to a migration from Korea) the cosmology became vertical and focused on the sun. There was an initial attempt to integrate the two world views by the sacred marriage of Amaterasu and Yamato, the female and male spirits. Soon, however, oracular possession by female shamans was discredited. It was replaced by the emperor's dreams which were interpreted by men. Then, too, a greater emphasis was placed on "vertical cosmology," male deities, and priests instead of priestesses. Eventually, the clan patron of the ruling house, Yamato Okami, assumed high god status and combined within himself sovereignty and fertility. Ellwood suggests that Amaterasu was "rediscovered" when the *Kojiki* and *Nihonshoki* were compiled during an age of several sovereign empresses (7th-8th centuries) who assumed the throne upon their husbands' death. "But even though Amaterasu was ... apotheosized to heaven, and sovereign empresses like these presided over the state and its rites below, society was now largely denatured of real *female* magic, mystery, or personality. Both Amaterasu and the empresses were figureheads in heavenly and earthly patriarchal orders, at best only sanctifying them with matriarchal tokens."[77]

The case of a more recent Near Eastern example, that of the Arabian peninsula, shows a slightly different kind of scenario. According to W. Montgomery Watt's reconstruction, much of Arabia prior to the advent of Islam was matrilineal.[78] More specifically, Bedouin clans were matrilineal. There were also signs of transition to patrilineality. By the time of Muhammad, Mecca had become patrilineal. The change, Watt argues, was bound up with the change from a nomadic to a settled economy, the growth of individualism, trade, private property, and urbanization. The Prophet championed the change to a patrilineal society, albeit with a number of safeguards for women's rights. While Muhammad never took on the mantle of supreme king, his political influence gradually extended as a result of his military victories and leadership. By the end of his life, he had become the most important person in Arabia. From a comparative perspective, we may expect a supreme male deity in the image of king to emerge with the change to a patrilineal society and with political unification.

Along with matrilineality, there had been some goddesses in Arabia prior to the advent of Islam. Al-'Uzzā, whose name means "The Strong, the Powerful" was associated with several sanctuaries and also with the morning star. Al-Lāt, which simply means "the goddess" also had her sanctuaries as did Manāt. The Meccans called them Allāh's daughters, though the relation between the old Arabian deity Allāh and these goddesses is far from clear. It has been suggested, however, that because they were popular and worshipped by powerful people, namely the Quraysh, that Muhammad may have decided at one point to incorporate them. Perhaps he was interested in gaining adherents where these goddesses were worshipped or perhaps the Quraysh in Mecca had made some kind of offer to the Prophet on condition that he acknowledge their deities. That he decided to acknowledge them is alluded to in the Qur'ān in the Sūrat an-Najm (53). These verses, however, were abrogated and came to be known as the Satanic Verses. Various versions of this episode are discussed by the traditional commentator, at-Ṭabarī. W. Montgomery Watt, after surveying all the evidence, says:

> The Qur'ān thus fits in with what we learnt from the traditional accounts. Muhammad must have had sufficient success for the heads of Quraysh to take him seriously. Pressure was brought to bear on him to make some acknowledgement of the worship at the neighbouring shrines. He was at first inclined to do so, both in view of the material advantages such a course offered and because it looked as if it would speedily result in a successful end to his mission. Eventually, however, through Divine guidance as he believed, he saw that this would be a fatal compromise, and he gave up the prospect of improving his outward circumstances in order to follow the truth as he saw it... If the stories of offers from the leading Quraysh are correct, then Muhammad must have been aware of the politi-

cal aspects of his decisions, and in particular of his promulgation of the satanic verses and of the abrogating verses. Likewise he must have been aware, when he finally rejected compromise by repeating Sūrat al-Kāfirīn, that there could be no peace with the Quraysh unless they accepted the validity of his mission.... The mention of the goddesses is thus properly the beginning of the active opposition of Quraysh, and Sūrat al-Kāfirīn, which seems so purely religious, made it necessary for Muḥammad to conquer Mecca.[79]

If Muḥammad did indeed incorporate the goddesses for a period of time, then this is another instance of an attempt to integrate goddesses but then to eliminate them. In the Arabian case, the development was internal in the sense that both Allāh and the goddesses had co-existed in the pre-Islamic period. The move toward a strict monotheism was also from within Arabian society. Another feature of the Arabian case was that the compromise of acknowledging both Allāh and the goddesses (after or during the development of strict monotheism) was for a very short period of time (Watt suggests several weeks or months). With Muhammad's consolidation of the Bedouin, the monotheistic religion spread. After the death of Muhammad, Allāh as supreme ruler paralleled the caliph as head of the empire. The names of Allāh, for instance, include al-Malik (The King), al-Mu'min (The Preserver of Security), al-Muhaymin (The Protector), al-Azīz (The Mighty), al-Jabbār (The Overpowering), al-Mutakabbir (The Great in Majesty, al-Qahhār (The Dominant), al-Kabīr (The Most Great), al-Qādir (The Powerful), al-Wālī (The Governor), Mālik al-Mulk (The Ruler of the Kingdom), and so forth.[80] Goddesses were gone, moreover, and matrilineality had virtually disappeared.

From the above discussion, it is clear that the pattern detected by Lerner was found (with variation) in other places. But was it universal? The answer simply is "no." We have no evidence, for example, of the prevalence of goddesses in neolithic proto-Indo-European sources. On the contrary, reconstruction of the proto-Indo-European language and mythology indicates that these people had patrilineal families, and worshipped a predominantly male pantheon. There was no need to change from goddesses to gods. There was a change, however, from many gods to the concept of a supreme ruler with many names and forms.

State formation can be correlated with emergence of patrilineality (where it had not previously existed) and dual-sex or male symbolism, leading eventually to male supreme deities. But the process was by no means uniform. Some cultural zones witnessed a change from matrilineality and goddess worship to patrilineality and supreme god worship (sometimes through an interim stage of sacred marriage between a god and goddess). Goddesses were marginalized in the sense that their creative functions no longer dominated the creation myths, were not central to definitions of political power, and became part of popular religion for specialized functions related to sickness and death, fertility and prosperity, esoteric knowledge and magic. This process sometimes occurred within a generation and sometimes took centuries. Other groups, however, changed from a pantheon of many male gods to a supreme male ruler. And still others transformed a *deus otiosus* into a supreme, active ruler.

Sanday suggests that symbolism may change when the economies change. But these changes occur in different ways. "If the transition to agriculture was a consequence of migration or conquest, people face the decision of whether to adopt or reject foreign supernatural symbols along with the new technology. The choice is clearly a function of circumstances."[81] Then, too, a group of hunters or warriors who migrate into an area of abundance where agriculture is practiced may change the mythological charter to incorporate both masculine and feminine symbolism whereas if resources are scarce, they may have "accentuated masculine-oriented origin myths."[82] With advanced plant economies and increasing technological complexity, there is a tendency toward a masculine orientation.[83]

In any case, can such developments be described as resulting, in the final analysis, from the reification and exploitation of the reproductive capacities of women as Lerner claims? While Lerner repudiates the theory that women are victims and men are victimizers — this enables her to claim that women are actors in history — she herself appropriates this view when giving her own explanation for the "patriarchal revolution." Although she suggests that a number of factors may have contributed to this revolution, she thinks that the reification of women's reproductive capacity was the root of their subordination. She thinks that this occurred with the development of agriculture and the rise of states. For her, the important point is that women's reproductive capacity was objectified and not men's. Women would bond to the new group through their children, would not use violence against their new group, would make better pawns in alliances with other tribes, and would help to increase the population more rapidly than men. Following Meillassoux, she says that:

> women's *biological vulnerability* in childbirth led
> tribes to procure more women from other groups
> and that this tendency toward the theft of women
> led to constant intertribal warfare. In the process,
> a warrior culture emerged. Another consequence
> of this theft of women is that the conquered
> women were protected by the men who had
> conquered them or by the entire conquering
> tribe. In the process, women were thought of as
> possessions, as things — they became reified —

while men became the reifiers because they
conquered and protected. Women's reproductive
capacity is first recognized as a tribal resource,
then, as ruling elites develop, it is acquired as
the property of a particular kin group. This
occurs with the development of agriculture.[84]

This is an odd argument. Since death in childbirth was
certainly nothing new for women at this time — it had always
been a danger — the need to replace women who died in childbirth can hardly be a reason for a warrior culture to emerge at
this particular moment. Because men and women are both
necessary for reproduction and a new infant needs care over an
extended period of time, human societies have always ordered
reproduction in some way. Even early human societies, for
instance, have guarded against incest. One way that this was
done was to take a partner from another band. It seems that at
first it was women who moved out of their natal band to seek
partners. Quale argues that even chimpanzees

> ... tend to move out toward other groups from
> their natal bands when they are receptive to
> intercourse ... It seems reasonable that expecting
> hominid females to move out, and hominid males
> to stay within the bands in which they had been
> born, would serve both incest avoidance (shown
> ... to be biologically advantageous) and the
> maintenance of bonds among groups of males
> who were accustomed to hunting together. It
> also seems reasonable that early hominid females
> would agree to such a move because they had
> recognized that collaborative hunting was more
> efficiently done by males who were familiar with
> one another as well as with the terrain, while
> females' gathering, though often done in com-

pany with one another, did not require as much
practiced cooperation as hunting ... It has been
hypothesized that brother-sister avoidance comes
naturally in human beings because of early
familiarity, which tends to preclude the feeling of
mild but discernible novelty that seems to be
required for strong and lasting attraction ... It
therefore seeems fairly likely that at least by the
time of Homo habilis a pattern had already been
established by which females left at maturity to
find mates in other bands, while males stayed
together as a hunting team.[85]

Thus, the movement of women from their natal band to that of
a non-kin band seems to be a very early development in human
history. A haphazard practice may have developed into an
orderly exchange of sisters between bands. The strategic
important of female kin in another band no doubt was recognized: related women may have helped to mediate larger-scale
hunting forays or resolve conflicts between the men of different
bands. All of this, thinks Quale, occurred early in human
prehistory (the time of *homo erectus* or even *homo habilis*).
Initiation of such an exchange of women, moreover, need not
be attributed to men. "It is worth emphasizing that both
females and males could have had equally good reasons to find
sister-exchanges preferable to having brothers be the ones to
move."[86] In short, the value of taking a partner from another
band was long recognized. This need not be explained by the
reification of women's reproductive capacity at the time of the
rise of states.

There is another problem with Lerner's reconstruction.
There had been a rapid development of population from the
time of the neolithic period to the rise of states in the ancient
Near East.

> As gathering began to move toward harvesting
> and storing, and then toward planting, which
> appears to be the probable order of development,
> more children began to survive to adulthood.
> The human population nearly doubled in the six
> thousand years after the first move toward agri-
> culture (in the sense of harvesting and storing),
> less than 12,000 years ago. It nearly doubled
> again in each of the next three millennia.[87]

It is possible that societies were more interested in checking this population growth than in increasing it. We cannot assume that tribes were stealing women from other groups because they wanted to increase their group's reproductive capacity.

It is also likely that the concept of private property stems from the neolithic development of the domestication of plants and animals. "By about 7000 B.C.... the pattern of separate sleeping huts and storage huts had changed to one of a single, separate sleeping and storage facility for each family. Clearly a sense of mine-and-thine was being inculcated."[88] Only with domestication was there the possibility of stockpiling important resources and the necessity of laying claim to them. Stockpiling resouces and the development of herds also made it possible for them to be exchanged or stolen. If there is a relation between the notion of private property and the reification of women, then one would expect this relation to develop in the neolithic period itself. This would challenge the notion of the neolithic period as a golden age for women. Or it would call for some other explanation of the subordination of women that seems to have occurred with the rise of states.

The rise of states is extremely complex. While I agree that it ushered in strong, if not extreme male domination, in the earliest phase, I find Lerner's explanation reductive. Although she mentions a number of explanations, she does not give importance to them in the final analysis. The subordination of

women had at least as much to do with the importance of male
biology (size, strength, and mobility) in plough agriculture,
trade, and war as it had to do with power. War objectified both
men (who were forced to fight and often lost their lives) and
women (who were captured and often raped). Although Lerner
is much more subtle than many authors and gives the appearance of judiciously assessing all theories, she manages to make
the exploitation of the reproductive capacities of women the
origin of all evil, including capitalism (since women are the
original private property) and slavery (since exploitation of the
reproductive labour of women provided the model for exploitation of male labour). What is this if not a version of the view
that women are the prototypical victims and men the prototypical victimizers?

Others have described these developments as a male rape
of nature, goddesses and women. In his foreward to *The
Language of the Goddess*, Campbell says that

> ... in contrast to the mythologies of the cattle-
> herding Indo-European tribes that, wave upon
> wave, from the fourth millennium B.C. overran
> the territories of Old Europe and whose male-
> dominated pantheons reflected the social ideals,
> laws, and political aims of the ethnic units to
> which they appertained, the iconography of the
> Great-Goddess arose in reflection and veneration
> of the laws of Nature. Gimbutas's lexicon of the
> pictorial script of that primordial attempt on
> humanity's part to understand and live in har-
> mony with the beauty and wonder of Creation
> adumbrates in archetypal symbolic terms a
> philosophy of human life that is in every aspect
> contrary to the manipulated systems that in the
> West have prevailed in historic times.

> One cannot but feel that in the appearance of this
> volume at just this turn of the century there is an
> evident relevance to the universally recognized
> need in our time for a general transformation of
> consciousness. The message here is of an actual
> age of harmony and peace in accord with the
> creative energies of nature which for a spell of
> some four thousand prehistoric years anteceded
> the five thousand of what James Joyce has
> termed the "nightmare" (of contending tribal and
> national interests) from which it is now certainly
> time for this planet to wake.[89]

Gimbutas traces the decline of the Old European world view to
invasions of the proto-Indo-Europeans between 4300 and 2800
B.C. which had the result, according to her introduction, of
"changing it from gylanic (i.e. egalitarian) to androcratic and
from matrilineal to patrilineal.... We are still living under the
sway of that aggressive male invasion and only beginning to
discover our long alienation from our authentic European
Heritage — gylanic, nonviolent, earth-centered culture."[90]
Her introduction is mild compared to her conclusion. There,
Gimbutas says that some symbols live on: "They could have
disappeared only with the *total extermination of the female
population.*"[91] This implies, of course, that women as a group
were systematically killed on a massive scale by men as part of
the male takeover.

> Parthenogenetic goddesses creating from them-
> selves without the help of male insemination
> gradually changed into brides, wives, and daugh-
> ters and were eroticized, linked with the prin-
> ciple of sexual love, as a response to a patriarch-
> al and patrilinear [sic] system.... Furthermore,
> Zeus had to "seduce" (with a nod toward histori-

cal accuracy, we might prefer the term "rape") hundreds of other goddesses and nymphs to establish himself....

[Later] the Killer-Regeneratrix, the overseer of cyclic life energy, the personification of winter, and Mother of the Dead, was turned into a witch of might and magic. In the period of the Great Inquisition, she was considered to be a disciple of Satan. The dethronement of this truly formidable goddess whose legacy was carried on by wise women, prophetesses, and healers who were the best and bravest minds of the time, is marked by blood and is the greatest shame of the Christian Church. The witch hunt of the 15th-18th centuries is a most satanic event in European history in the name of Christ. The murder of women accused as witches escalated to more than eight million.... This was the beginning of the dangerous convulsions of androcratic rule which 460 years later reached the peak in Stalin's East Europe with the torture and murder of fifty million women, children, and men.

The Old European culture was the matrix of much later beliefs and practices. Memories of a long-lasting gynocentric past could not be erased, and it is not surprising that the feminine principle plays a formidable role in the subconscious dream and fantasy world. It remains (in Jungian terminology) "the repository of human experience" and a "depth structure." To an archeologist it is an extensively documented historical reality.[92]

It is striking that whereas in other places Gimbutas speaks of gylanic (egalitarian) rule, here she shows her hand and speaks unabashedly of a *gynocentric* past. She has said in an interview that "'Our authentic European heritage' was a nonviolent, earth-avowing culture where 'the ruling was in the women's hands.'"[93] All of history since the Indo-European invasion of Old Europe represents the evil ways of men. Whereas other feminists have spoken of "the ultimate hubris, symbolic matricide by setting up an all-masculine theology"[94] and have insinuated a male conspiracy theory, Gimbutas speaks of the actual murder, rape and extermination of women. In fact, the warrior tones of her moral indignation are akin to the rage of Mary Daly who speaks of the 1980s as

> ... a period of extreme danger for women and for our sister the earth and her other creatures, all of whom are targeted by the maniacal fathers, sons, and holy ghosts for extinction by nuclear holocaust, or, failing that, by chemical contamination, by escalated ordinary violence, by man-made hunger and disease that proliferate in a climate of deception and mind-rot.

> Yet at this very time, somehow living/longing through, above, before, and beyond it, thousands of women struggle to re-member ourselves and our history, to sustain and intensify a biophilic identified bonding and creation, we refuse to turn back. For those who survive in the only real sense, that is, with metapatriarchal consciousness alive and growing, our struggle and quest concern Elemental participation in Be-ing. Our passion is for that which is most intimate and most ultimate, for depth and transcendence, for recalling original wholeness. In Naming/reclaim-

ing passionate Elemental knowing, knowing that is intuitive/immediate, not mediated by the omnipresent myths of phallicism, we call forth hope and courage to transcend appearance....

In some ways, *Pure Lust* can be seen as the parthenogenetic daughter of those earlier works...

The weapons of Wonderlusting women are the Labryses/double axes of our own Wild wisdom and wit, which cut through the mazes of man-made mystification, breaking the mindbindings of master-minded doublethink.... Recognizing that deep damage has been inflicted upon consciousness under phallocracy's myths and institutions, we continue to Name patriarchy as the perverted paradigm and source of other social evils....

This commitment implies experience and understanding of the Goddess as Metaphor.[95]

But does this view of history do justice to all the facts? Gimbutas and others presume that the neolithic age was peaceful and the rise of states violent. This is an oversimplification. We have already noted evidence for human sacrifice in neolithic societies. Sacrifice, animal or human, was hardly peaceful or, for that matter, natural. Gimbutas has said "It's a fact that these people lived in much happier times."[96] But we must not forget that people then faced numerous problems such as drought, plagues, a very short life span, death in childbirth and a host of other problems. To dismiss such problems is sheer romanticism. Nature itself was often feared; long after the neolithic period the wilderness was perceived as dangerous.

As we have noted before, only with domestication of plants and animals was there the possibility of stockpiling

important resources. Raiding may have developed within both
pastoral and agricultural communities. It cannot be argued,
then, that the proto-Indo-Europeans were violent by nature; any
group could have developed a more warlike nature, especially
if resources were few. In fact, the most recent theory is that the
Indo-Europeans themselves were originally agriculturalists.
Colin Renfrew, who is Disney Professor of Archaeology at the
University of Cambridge, challenges Gimbutas' reconstruction
of an Indo-European (Kurgan) invasion:

> Drawing on the evidence described by Childe
> and buttressing it with recent findings, Gimbutas
> reconstructed a series of "Kurgan invasions"
> flowing west from the lands north of the Black
> Sea ... Yet to my mind it is not a satisfactory
> story. My reasoning is several fold. In the first
> place, the archaeology is not convincing ...
> Perhaps the strongest objection is simply the lack
> of conviction behind the whole story. Why on
> earth should hordes of mounted warriors have
> moved west at the end of the Neolithic, subjugat-
> ing the inhabitants of Europe and imposing the
> proto-Indo-European language on them? What
> enormous upsurge of population on the steppes
> could have been responsible? Although its
> construction is elegant, the story does not ring
> true for this listener.[97]

Renfrew, after discussing alternative evidence and interpretations (including the process of cultural and linguistic change),
argues that people from Anatolia (rather than the Russian
steppes) gradually migrated (from about 6500 B.C.) west. They
went to Greece, then the Balkans, central Europe and southern
Italy bringing the knowledge of agriculture with them. Local

inhabitants would have adopted agriculture from the immigrants.
Refrew thinks that:

> there is considerably greater continuity in Euro-
> pean prehistory than has previously been believed
> ... In this light the whole early history of Europe
> appears as a series of transformations and evol-
> utionary adaptations on a common proto-Indo-
> European base augmented by a few non-Indo-
> European survivals. The story is not predicated
> on a series of migrations from without but on a
> series of complex interactions within a Europe
> that was already fundamentally agricultural in
> economy and Indo-European in language.[98]

Renfrew's alternative hypothesis challenges the conspiracy view
of history in no uncertain terms. We can now argue that
archaeological evidence of a warrior culture which emerged in
Old Europe reflected the internal development of an agricultual
peoples — perhaps related to the growing population, which
created pressure on land and resources — rather than an
invasion of a violent, foreign group as Gimbutas claims. In
short, the Indo-Europeans were not by nature a violent people
who disturbed the life of a peaceful culture.

It also cannot be argued that men are violent by nature.
If that were the case, there would have been constant raiding
and warfare already in hunting and gathering societies.
Violence did increase in some pastoral and agricultural societies
(if Renfrew's hypothesis is accepted). Raiding also led to a
"heroic ethos of male valour" in some areas. And this, in turn,
stimulated the development of states. But such violence was
related to new cultural developments, not to biology itself.
Moreover, there is ample evidence that women cheered men on
in the raids and battles. They also fought on occasion.[99]
Victory provided more resources, power, and honour for

women as well as men, even though it sometimes involved
massive loss of human life (which especially affected men) or
capture (which especially affected women). To cite just one
example, consider the following South Indian (Tamil) heroic
poem from the Caṅkam period about a man who lost his life
killing the elephant of an opposing warrior in battle.

> When she learned her son had died killing an
> elephant,
> the joy of the old woman,
> her hair pure grey like the feathers of a fish-eating
> heron,
> was greater than the day she bore him;
> her tears were more
> than the drops that quiver on strong bamboo
> on Mount Vetiram
> after a rain.[100]

George L. Hart, who translated this poem, discusses the
woman's identification with the heroism of her husband or son
in the following terms:

> The reason the mother rejoices when she learns
> that her son has died a hero is that she is ulti-
> mately responsible for his heroism in that she has
> passed on to him her own power.... By seeing
> that her son has died a hero, the mother realizes
> that she has succeeded in her aim, and that she
> has been able to impart enough of her power to
> her son to enable him to find what was for the
> Tamils (at least in theory) the greatest fulfillment
> a man could find, a heroic death in battle. The
> mother's happiness at such an outcome is even
> more vividly described in Pur. 295, where her
> breasts flow with milk again when she sees the

> heroic death of her son ... [wives] are thrilled at
> the wounds of their dead husbands.[101]

We are reminded that many goddesses after the rise of the state were goddesses of war. Ishtar, for example, was praised "as mistress of the battlefield, more powerful than kings, more powerful than other gods."[102] Lerner adds: "My point here is that men and women offering such prayers when in distress must have thought of women, just as they thought of men, as capable of metaphysical power."[103] Thus, when the subject is the power of women as reflected in goddesses, women are quite willing to appropriate these images. When they are arguing that women are peaceful by nature, however, they ignore the warrior nature of many goddesses such as Ishtar, Athena, and Durgā.[104]

Despite the massive loss of life, it is only fair to note that the rise of states must have been an attractive proposition for human societies. Had this not been so, the experiment would not have been repeated. Many early states, for instance, were extremely fragile structures and collapsed with slight shocks such as drought or disruption of trade routes. In this context, it is instructive to recall how the collapse of the Chou dynasty in China led to the long, brutal, and anarchic Warring States Period. Confucius advocated a return to the state and rule by benevolence; for him, the ideal man was not the warrior, however, but the *ch'ün tzu*, the gentleman. Even though his view of society may not look that attractive to us today — and we must not confuse his vision with that which was implemented in his name during the Han dynasty — it was still an important and peaceful vision for his period of time. Such examples could be multiplied. We often find, for example, that the early experiments with ruthless power so often symbolized as omnipotence were gradually curtailed. The concept of an omnipotent king gave way to the concept of a just king. Capturing enemy women by force — whether to punish the enemy or to define the warrior's status — was severely criticized. Marriage as gift came to replace marriage as seizure. Similarly, symbolic rituals such as the offering of fruits and flowers replaced animal and human sacrifice in many areas. Infanticide and a host of other aggressive acts were criticized, legally prohibited, and punished as crimes. The historical record is certainly uneven. But religions such as Brahmanical Hinduism, Buddhism, and Jainism (which were reforms of Indo-European religion after the rise of the state) did proclaim the principle of non-injury (*ahimsā*). Subsequent history can be read as an attempt to extend this principle into more and more areas of life. Just as Gimbutas points to the darkest events in history (such as those associated with Stalin), so others can point to the bright ones (such as those associated with Mahatma Gandhi) which help to sustain and work toward a vision of a better world. And if a goddess lives on in the Virgin Mary (something Gimbutas herself claims), goddesses — some as wives and some as independent supreme beings who create, preserve and destroy the cosmos like their male counterparts — also appeared in the Indo-European pantheon with the development of stable states.

Conclusion

Is it a coincidence that such views of history resemble the Western paradigm of the fall from paradise? According to Julien Ries,

> Within historical time, it is very close to the beginnings of time conceived as a golden age in contrast to which the fall and its consequences represent a break or degradation.... The theogonic aspect of the fall deals with the degradation of the divine and is found in the numerous myths

concerning the origin of the gods, of their victory over chaos, or of the victory of the more
recent forces of divinity over older ones. Coextensive with the creation, the fall as presented
in theogony implies the identification of evil and
chaos on the one hand and of salvation and
creation on the other.... Anthropogony, however, offers the most important perspective on
the fall. From this perspective, the contemporary human condition — a condition of degra-
dation in contrast to that of the golden age of
humanity — is explained as the consequence of
a fall, a tragic event that bursts into human
history.... Myths of the fall clearly show three
essential elements: (1) the concept of a golden
age in the beginning, (2) ... a break or degra-
dation of original harmony, (3) the explanation
of the present human condition ... any conception of the fall has implications concerning the
origins of evil, as well as intimations of a possible overcoming of evil through a recovery of the
state that existed previous to the fall. Thus ...
[an] ethical dimension is grafted onto, and is
coextensive with, the idea of the fall and forms
an important part of a hermeneutical approach
that tries to come to terms with its relationship to
guilt or fault.[105]

In the Judaeo-Christian tradition, paradise means living together
in harmony with God and the created world. During the
neolithic period, according to some feminists, people lived in
harmony with the Goddess and the natural world. As Ries
observes, the Bible[106] notes "humanity's corruption, variously
described as fratricidal war, polygamy, desert warfare, or the
division of nations and tongues ... [when evil] is born in the

hearts of men and always remains at the heart of history, an inevitable force in human affairs."[107]   Similarly, Western women who are devotees of the Goddess today believe that the rise of the state was coeval with the advent of war, nationalism, and the forcible abduction of women to exploit their reproductive labour through polygamy.   According to the account in Genesis, a woman initiated the Fall; according to some feminist theories, the fall from primeval peace and harmony was initiated by men.   But the Biblical account[108] holds *both* Adam and Eve responsible and punishes both since *both* acted against the will of God.   The feminist account blames only men.   The new version, then, pits moral woman against immoral man.

By relating current goddess worship to history, our authors indicate their deep roots in Western civilization — which they themselves have denounced as a patriarchal order. Despite their celebration of nature, they are profoundly historical in orientation.   This should come as no surprise since Western religions look to God acting within history.   Similarly, we have seen that the historical model they use is similar to the Biblical account of the Fall from paradise.   Just as the Biblical God is omnipotent, a supreme king, so "The Great Goddess" is omnipotent, a supreme queen.   Then, too, just as the supreme God creates alone, so does "The Great Goddess."   She is considered parthenogenic.   While omnipotence, supremacy, and parthenogenesis mirror the patriarchal concept of a supreme deity, it is hardly coincidental — but highly ironic — that these terms also reflect current feminist interest in power, superiority, and reproductive autonomy.

More importantly, we have raised the question of non-scholarly or hidden agendas.   Some of our authors have been blunt about the matter and have admitted their ulterior motives. In her comments on feminist methodology, Elizabeth Schüssler Fiorenza writes: "The notion of objective and disinterested research must be replaced by *conscious partiality*... Rather than reproducing the scholarly rhetoric of impartiality and value-neutrality, feminist biblical scholars need to spell out our commitments and challenge our colleagues to do the same."[109] Most of the above scholars have spelled out their commitments. But does this make their work scholarly? Does merely acknowledging bias legitimate it? If some feminists think that they can achieve legitimacy for gynocentrism merely by identifying it as such, why should men not do the same for androcentrism? The answer to this last question, according to some feminists, is that they are merely doing what men have already done. But this is an inadequate answer. We have only recently become aware of androcentrism. In earlier times, that kind of bias was the result of assumptions that were seldom challenged. Succumbing to bias unconsciously is one thing; consciously *choosing* bias is something else. The latter is hypocritical and opportunistic. It leads to cynicism. I base this claim on both logical and moral grounds. If it is wrong for men to do something, it is wrong for women to do the same thing. And no context can turn something which is wrong or false into something which is right or true. Even oppressed people, after all, can acknowledge intellectual and moral standards that transcend their own experience. Being oppressed does not give them *carte blanche* to say or do anything at all. Otherwise, terrorists could legitimate their behaviour merely by pointing to their version of history which revolves around the wrongs inflicted upon them. In doing so, of course, they would reduce both scholarship and morality to sheer expediency. The end, I argue, does *not* justify the means.

By definition, scholarship is based on the assumption that attaining some level of objective knowledge is possible. From this, it follows that scholars must account, to the best of their ability, for demonstrable facts. As finite beings, of course, they cannot expect to produce results which are more than provisional; other scholars may come along with new information or new interpretations which more fully explain the facts. Nevertheless, the scholarly enterprise must assume that there is knowledge of the external world to be sought in the first place. Otherwise, they are playing intellectual games. Some feminists, however, try to legitimate their bias by arguing that objectivity in scholarship is impossible. It is true, of course, that complete objectivity is impossible. Does that mean we should stop striving for it? In that case, we should embrace totalitarianism on the grounds that perfect democracy is impossible. But why should we adopt this all-or-nothing mentality? To the extent that such feminists deny the very existence of objective truth, they reject scholarship itself. At the very least, honesty should compel them to abandon the claim to being scholars. They may be doing something valuable or even necessary. But it is not scholarship. If we accept the idea that there is no point in seeking objective knowledge or truth, moreover, ethical responsibility should compel us to disband all universities. After all, why should the public be defrauded and forced to pay for useless institutions? If we acknowledge, however, that there *are* objective criteria for knowledge, then we should not expect universities to hire those who openly reject the *sine qua non* of scholarship. It could be argued that intellectual life is now under siege not by the masses (as in the past) but by the academics. Special interest groups view themselves as immune to any standards of judgment. They ignore facts that contradict their own view. They attack canons of scholarly proof. And they circumvent reason by asking: *Whose* truth? *Whose* standards? *Whose* logic? Any challenge may be shrugged off as the view of a traitor to the cause or merely as a reflection of the dominant culture (which, by the very fact of its dominance, is evil).

One of the inspirations for such relativism has been the movement called Deconstruction. According to this school of thought, all positions are relative, for they are interrelated as the words of a sentence. They are constructs which can be *de*constructed.

> The concept of thing, substance, event, and
> absolute recedes, to be superseded by the concept
> of relation, ratio, construct, and relativity....
> Once one realizes that what seems to be an event
> is really a construct of a quasi-linguistic system,
> then one is in a position to undo the construct or
> to recognize that the construct, by its very
> nature, has already undone, dismantled, or
> deconstructed itself — with far-reaching implica-
> tions for thought of every sort.[110]

According to Jacques Derrida, the chief exponent of
Deconstruction, a close reading of a text reveals crucial
oppositions: nature-culture, chaos-order, speech-writing, reason-
rhetoric, *logos-mimesis*, literal-figurative, male-female, and so
forth. It also reveals how they are hierarchically ordered. One
term is unprivileged or subordinate because it is a derivative or
supplement (an optional extra or a necessary addition); the other
is privileged and dominant. He then shows how this relation
can, in fact, be inverted. As a result, the subordinate term has
priority.

  Derrida has analyzed the relations of men and women in
this manner. In his study of Hegel, for instance, he has shown
how dialectic is inscribed within a system of self-regulating
concepts and values. According to Christopher Norris, it is a
system which

> ... connects in turn with the sexual division of
> labour where reason is exclusively a male pre-
> rogative, a power exercised by virtue of the
> husband's joint access to the domestic and civil
> spheres, while woman remains duty-bound to her
> role as wife, mother and family helpmeet (sic).
> Derrida goes various ways around to deconstruct
> this covert gender-politics everywhere at work in

the texts of Hegelian philosophy. He incorporates passages on love, marriage and the family from Hegel's letters and other biographical material; examines the way that his reading of Sophocles' *Antigone* turns upon this same dialectical overcoming of woman's interests in the name of male reason and political order. He then goes on to show, through a series of elaborately staged intertextual readings, how other philosophers (including Kant) have likewise managed to repress or to sublimate woman's voice while claiming to speak in the name of universal humanity and absolute reason. All this in counterpoint with the passages from Genet (chiefly *Our Lady of the Flowers* and *The Thief's Journal* which supply not so much an ironic gloss as an adversary language which progressively invades and disfigures the discourse of Hegelian reason. Thus *Glas* opens up the domain of male dialectical thought to a series of complicating detours and aporias that cannot be subsumed by any logic of speculative reason.[111]

In this manner, Derrida exposes the Western gender system. This is part of his larger project of questioning the grounds of various truth-claims, revealing the assumptions of Western ethnocentric and logocentric discourse, and revealing its constitutive blind-spots.

Many feminists have found Derrida's strategies very useful. They identify the derivative or the supplement with women, "The Goddess," and women's oral tradition in patriarchal society. They expose the privileged position of men, God, and androcentric discourse and speak of this as a conspiracy or male takeover. And they then invert the terms so that women, "The Goddess," and feminist discourse have priority (biologically, historically, and morally). Goldenberg, for instance, urges people to focus on feminine images of power and to deconstruct central images of patriarchal authority, which resulted from a male conspiracy:

> To teach that Judaism and Christianity arose out of pagan cultural contexts which granted women a great deal of prominence certainly in their mythologies and possibly in their hierarchies, is to teach that Judaism and Christianity had political motives for their early rejection and denigration of female imagery. This approach to religious history makes it possible for many people to see female imagery living on in dominant traditions. Women are there. Things female are there. But they have been *inverted or cloaked over in order to be appropriated by male phallic history and mythology.*[112]

Goddess "thealogy," notes Goldenberg, also speaks of the need to replace the Father, Son and Holy Ghost with Diana, Luna, and Hecate. The shift from an interest in male symbols poses a challenge to the importance of the father. The so-called solid male institutions are not solid; there are cracks in the edifice. Whereas once men argued that the penis represents power, now it is argued that the glorification of the penis is really only the result of frustrated desire to return to the mother and overcome the original separation from her breast. Whereas once there were separate spheres based on the distinction of the political realm and the home, now there are none because "the personal is political." And whereas once disembodied concepts or abstractions were preferred, now all knowledge is viewed as embodied. From Goldenberg's discussion we can see the method of inversion at work.

Opponents of Deconstruction have said that this method leads to relativism and a "corresponding elevation of the Empty Man, the nomadic 'man without qualities' who can weave his way through all hierarchies showing them to be temporary and nonsensical."[113]   It is certainly true that for Derrida Deconstruction is an elusive method: he cannot know what it is, how it works, or what the results will be. Having inverted the terms and demonstrated the intertextual echos, moreover, he implies that he has finished his exercise. It is time to move on. Language is, after all, only a "differential structure of contrasts and relationships without positive terms ... [and] meaning is endlessly deferred along the chain of linguistic substitutions and displacements that occur whenever we seek to define what a given term signifies in context."[114]   Derrida says that he looks for the surplus of meaning in metaphors, allusions, and other figures of speech. This enables him to move away from the rigidity and value structure of the oppositions. Presumably, he would be concerned that the inversion of gender relations not be frozen into an ideological position of good versus evil or woman versus man. This, after all, would be the reassertion of an opposition. But Derrida also suggests that by staying close to the text, he avoids the possibility of anomie. Moreover, he speaks of the redemptive value of his criticism. Here we are reminded of his statement of purpose: to question Western assumptions and ethnocentrism. (Presumably, gender assumptions would be included.) Thus, it seems that Derrida must be harbouring some assumptions of his own. These, in fact, may determine what texts he *selects* for deconstruction. Redemption implies, after all, something positive; one must be saved from something.

Feminists such as those we have been discussing, however, do not reject the notion of objective knowledge out of hand. They do so only when it suits them, that is, when they cannot rely on verifiable facts to support their claims. Unlike Derrida, who walks a fine line between relativism and redemption, they are quite clear about the danger of relativism for their own cause. They use the methods of Deconstruction only to prove that patriarchal texts are inherently privileged and unstable. They are not willing to deconstruct the inversion of gender once insight into male privilege and the hegemony of androcentric discourse has been gained. They are convinced of the political nature of gender and the need to improve the status of women through inversion of the hierarchy. They attempt, therefore, to prevent further deconstruction of feminist interpretations by arguing that it is necessary to redress the harm created by male evil, both past and present.

To redress such harm, therapy is necessary. Goddess "thealogians," according to Goldenberg, encourage a connection to the past (a goddess at the beginning of the universe) for the purpose of heightening involvement in the present (goddess worship today). Drawing on object relations theory which emphasizes the mother at the beginning of an individual's psychic universe, Goddess "thealogians" presuppose a connection between prehistory and the deep background of our psychological lives. When this connection is made conscious or ritually recalled (as a kind of eternal return), it is therapeutic because it creates psychological distance from patriarchal symbols and customs.[115] *It is not necessary to be absolutely scholarly about the past. Fantasy about the past* can also empower women in the present.

> In addition to employing fantasy in religious practice, Goddess thealogians also use it to 'do thealogy,' that is, to theorize about the Goddess. Sometimes the idea of a matriarchy in the past is put forward as a wish about history — a wish to be realized in the present and future. Thealogians are fond of quoting these lines of Monique Wittig from *Les Guérillères*: "There was a time when you were not a slave, remember. Try hard

to remember. Or, failing that, invent." The
wisdom of the words lies in the recognition that
belief in a state of beneficence that existed in the
past is an idea which empowers in the present.
Wittig recommends *that an invented past can be
substituted for a remembered one.* After all, she
implies, faith is simply a very strong wish.[116]

Object relations theory may have opened the door for understanding fantasy as history, but it is Goldenberg who has made
the link explicit. From this perspective, if one wishes there
were matriarchy in the past and writes about it as if it were
true, then this is sufficient for therapy; people "build their 'real'
worlds ... to correspond to their deepest inner expectations."[117]

Instead of conceiving of a fairly separate line
between "reality thinking" and "fantasy thinking," as did Freud and many of his followers,
object relations analysts conceive of fantasy as
the basis or context of all thinking. What is felt
to be real in the inner, psychic world, they say,
tends to be what is created in the external world.
Fantasy is seen as determining the blueprint of a
life.... These analysts, therefore, like many
witches, see the entire external, human world as
something constructed upon a stratum of internal
fantasy ... they both maintain that the inner
world of anticipation and wish is the basis of all
human thought and action.[118]

Goldenberg says that both "thealogians" and analysts "understand fantasy or wish as constituting the primary matrix for all
mental processes."[119] Feminists who follow this line of
thinking are willing to recover so-called historical truth from the

past when it legitimates their own views and proves therapeutic. When it does not, however, they resort to fantasy. If it is said that fantasy is the basis for all thinking and the external world is constructed on a stratum of internal fantasy, then it becomes very easy to claim fiction as fact. But what does this mean for scholarship? Anyone, of course, can create fantasies and try to convince others that they are true. But does this *make* them true? Is there any place for the knowledge provided by the history of religions and other disciplines? Or, in an age of deconstruction, is the very concept of knowledge something relegated to the past?

It is certainly true that scholarship has been closely related to the Enlightenment task of discovering truth. The facts are gathered, interpreted and sometimes explained. In the field of history of religions, scholars have been trained to reduce distortion caused by the superimposition of their own world view on the facts by the practice of *epoché*, bracketing out through self-consciousness of their own biases. While they admit that this is not always completely successful, they know well the improvement in scholarship when this method is sincerely attempted. A comparison with reports on Hinduism by 19th century missionaries, for instance, and contemporary scholarship by historians of religions makes this only too clear despite current charges of Orientalism and the usual scholarly debates within the discipline itself. Historians of religions have also tried to ensure an adequate basis for generalizations by detecting patterns from a representative sample of societies throughout space and time. Likewise, social anthropologists have tried to correct for distortions by searching for patterns on the basis of a large sample rather than a single society. They, too, have confidence that this method yields significant insights on human societies despite challenges to specific conclusions. In short, there remains a confidence at the core of such kinds of scholarship that knowledge about the past can grow and that there are standards for the collection of data and its interpretation, even though these need to be periodically reviewed.

There is another problem with making fantasy "the basis or context of all thinking." If women claim that indulging in fantasies of a male conspiracy against women is an avenue to knowledge or a means of therapy, men could claim that fantasies of a female conspiracy against men have the same advantages. In that case, there could be nothing wrong with the pornography women now find so appalling. And there would be nothing wrong with *The Protocols of the Elders of Zion*[120] which purports to be the secret minutes of a Jewish organization plotting to takeover the world.

This particular feminist world view also has some serious problems. First, where is the self-criticism of such feminists to come from?[121] In the Biblical tradition, there is a transcendent source of ethical authority which dispenses both grace and judgment. *Everyone* is to be judged, men and women alike. But who is to judge "conscious partiality" if there is no transcendent authority or criteria by which to evaluate truth? The claim that there is no objective truth really means that, for all practical purposes, "anything goes." Does this not amount to a claim of infallibility? Then, too, some feminists have argued that men are really worshipping themselves when they worship a male deity. Could the same not be said of women who worship a female deity?

What if such feminist reconstructions of history result in the profound alienation of men? The idea that men as a group are biologically redundant or inherently evil can only be profoundly alienating for them. That goddess worship seems to be reserved exclusively for women seeking therapy or "woman-space," moreover, can only exacerbate this alienation. This is a much more radical form of exclusion than exclusion from the priesthood or from leadership positions in churches. If the lives of women and men are inextricably linked in both the private and public spheres — which they surely are for most people —

then how can such arguments possibly lead to anything but further polarization between men and women?   I am not opposed to the worship of female deities. But I am not opposed to the worship of male deities either.   In the first place, I understand the importance of religious and cultural continuity. Religious traditions are extremely fragile at this moment in history despite their endurance over a long period of time. There is a good deal of human wisdom embedded in these traditions.   They also provide visions of an ordered yet self-critical world at a time of rapid social change.   Therefore, it may be important to protect them while reforming them.   Then, too, I am sympathetic to the traditional boundaries of mono-theism. It is laudable that much feminine symbolism was incor-porated into the scriptural imagery of supreme male deities. It is not so laudable that current views on goddesses have ignored masculine attributes, have appropriated them without acknowl-edging their masculine origin, or claim these attributes as bad in male deities but good in female ones.   And I person-ally think that the idea of God as a caring, benevolent, and just father is extremely important, especially at a time when the notion of fatherhood is trivialized and when family violence is escalating.

As a historian of religions, I am aware that female symbolism increased in many stable states when there was little stress. Even without the feminist desire to deconstruct patri-archy, goddesses and divine couples became popular. Supreme male deities developed feminine attributes and sometimes (as in the case of Śiva) androgynous forms. But this only happened, I suspect, when masculine identity was secure. Current promo-tion of goddesses is historically unprecedented in its female exclusivity and its hostility toward men. As such, it is closer to ideology than religion.

Karl Marx wanted to expose the hidden assumptions of Western culture and show that they were creations of the cultural order and not givens of the natural order. He also wanted to show how assumptions were propagated by the dominant class in order to perpetuate its power. Thinking that there was a conspiracy of the privileged against the unprivileged, he wanted to destroy it by exposing it and empowering the oppressed. For Marx, then, the world was divided into two categorically different groups. Evil was associated with one; good with the other. Justice was the triumph of the powerless over the powerful, of the good over the wicked. Now, though, men are identified as privileged and therefore wicked. Women, on the other hand, are identified as unprivileged and therefore good. Justice, therefore, is the triumph of women over men. Such a view may be understood as an ideological form of feminism; the old sexual hierarchy has merely been stood on its head. Like all world views, of course, it can be subject to criticism. But that would mean taking scholarship on goddesses, theology and ethics seriously.

** I would like to thank my colleagues, Dr. Paul Nathanson of the McGill Centre for Medicine, Ethics, and Law and Leslie Orr of the Faculty of Religious Studies, McGill University, for their valuable comments.

Notes

1. Gerda Lerner, *The Creation of Patriarchy* (New York: Oxford University Press, 1986).

2. Lerner 222.

3. Lerner 228.

4. Marija Gimbutas, *The Language of the Goddess* (San Francisco: Harper & Row, 1989).

5. Patricia McGee, "Challenging history: Peaceful women may have once ruled the world," *Macleans*, 103:7 (1990), 66-67.

6. By Old European Gimbutas means the area extending from the Aegean and Adriatic to Czechoslovakia, southern Poland and the western Ukraine between 7000 and 3500 B.C.

7. Lerner does add a caveat: "The hypothetical construct I will offer is intended only as one of a number of possible models . . . Since we will most likely never know just what happened, we are constrained to speculate on what might have been possible" (Lerner 38).

8. Lerner 148-149.

9. Lerner 39.

10. Lerner 39.

11. Lerner 40.

12. Naomi R. Goldenberg, "The return of the Goddess: Psychoanalytic reflections on the shift from theology to thealogy," *Studies in Religion*, 16:1 (1987), 39-41.

13. Goldenberg 41.

14. Gimbutas xix.

15. Karl J. Narr, "Paleolithic Religion," *The Encyclopedia of Religion*, ed. Mircea Eliade (New York: Macmillan, 1987), 5.

16. Peggy Reeves Sanday, *Female Power and Male Dominance: On the Origins of Sexual Inequality* (Cambridge: Cambridge University Press, 1981).

17. Sanday 68.

18. Sanday 66.

19. Gimbutas 317.

20. Gimbutas 3.

21. Gimbutas 259.

22. Gimbutas 258-263.

23. Gimbutas 175.

24. Lerner 33.

25. Lerner 148-149.

26. Barbara G. Walker, *The Woman's Encyclopedia of Myths and Secrets* (San Francisco: Harper & Row 1983), 346.

27. Gimbutas xv.

28. Gimbutas 316.

29. Gimbutas xix.

30. Gimbutas 318-319.

31. Of course, the deity Śiva is another example of this process in the Indian context.

32. Gimbutas 175.

33. Gimbutas 181.

34. Gimbutas 230-231.

35. Gimbutas 231.

36. Gimbutas 232.

37. Gimbutas 265.

38. Gimbutas 232.

39. Gimbutas 196, emphasis added.

40. Gimbutas 265.

41. Gimbutas 265.

42. Gimbutas 265.

43. Gimbutas 266.

44. Susan G.E. Frayser, *Varities of Sexual Experience: An Anthropological Perspective on Human Sexuality* (New Haven: HRAS Press, 1985), 284. Carl Ernst von Baer first observed the ovum in 1827.

45. Frayser 286-288.

46. Lerner 17.

47. G. Robina Quale, *A History of Marriage Systems* (New York: Greenwood Press, 1988), 29.

48. Lerner 39, emphasis added.

49. Lerner 42. Lerner also suggests that children and women hunt small animals. It is difficult to accept this as the case, for it would mean that men in areas where there was no large game hunting would have no function in the society in palaeolithic or neolithic times. Evidence suggests that there was some functional division of labour between men and women.

50. Lerner 45.

51. R.G. Edwards, "Chromosomal Abnormalities in Human Embryos," *Nature*, 303:5915 (1983), 283.

52. Jeremy Cherfas and John Gribbin, *The Redundant Male: Is Sex Irrelevant in the Modern World* (New York: Pantheon Books, 1984).

53. Lerner 49.

54. Gimbutas xx.

55. Gimbutas xx, emphasis added.

56. Gimbutas xiii, emphasis added.

57. Lerner 47, emphasis added.

58. Lerner 49, emphasis added.

59. Lerner 30, quoting Martin and Voorhies, *Female of the Species*. In her footnote she also notes the evidence of David Aberle reported in "Matrilineal Descent in Cross-cultural Perspective," in Kathleen Gough and David Schneider, eds. *Matrilineal Kinship* (Berkeley: University of California Press, 1961) 657-727. According to his study of 101 hunter-gatherer, 79 pastoral, 188 hoe-agricultural, and 117 plough-agricultural societies, 56% of

all matrilineal societies practice hoe-agriculture. But only 25% of hoe-agricultural groups are matrilineal (37% being bilateral, 35% patrilineal, and 3% duolineal). Thus, this study shows that bilaterality and patrilineality are the dominant practices rather than just patrilineality. Be that as it may, the point here is that not all or even most hoe-agricultural societies are matrilineal and hoe-agricultural societies are comparatively few.

60. Sanday 269.

61. Lerner 35.

62. Lerner 29.

63. David M. Schneider and Kathleen Gough, *Matrilineal Kinship* (Berkeley: University of California Press, 1961), 22.

64. A.R. Radcliffe-Brown and Daryll Forde, *African Systems of Kinship and Marriage* (London: Oxford University Press, 1950), 283-284.

65. Schneider and Gough 22.

66. Karla O. Poewe, *Matrilineal Ideology: Male-Female Dynamics in Luapula, Zambia* (London: Academic Press, 1981), 50.

67. Poewe 61.   Poewe also notes that "Some men are obsessed with the sexual activities of their wife.   They might spend days scheming how to catch their wife and her lover during sexual intercourse.... Usually, [the] duration [of conflict] ... is shortened by outbursts of physical violence.... Of 250 civil court cases heard in

Lukwesa during the year 1973, 103 refer to tensions between the sexes" (69).

68. Gimbutas 223.

69. Quale 33.

70. Lerner 53.

71. Lerner 144-146.

72. Lerner 151.

73. See Robert van Gulik. *La vie sexuelle dans la Chine ancienne* (Paris: Gallimard, 1971), 28.

74. Gulik 28.

75. Sanday 68-69.

76. Robert S. Ellwood, "Patriarchal Revolution in Ancient Japan: Episodes from the Nihonshoki Sujin Chronicle," *Journal of Feminist Studies in Religion*, 2:2 (1989).

77. Ellwood 34.

78. W. Montgomery Watt, *Muhammad at Medina* (Oxford: Clarendon Press, 1956), 378-388.

79. W. Montgomery Watt, *Muhammad at Mecca*, (Oxford: Clarendon Press, 1953), 108-109.

80. S.G.F. Brandon, *A Dictionary of Comparative Religion* (New York: Macmillan, 1970), 306-307.

81. Sanday 70.

82. Sanday 72.

83. Sanday 69.

84. Lerner 49.

85. Quale 30-33.

86. Quale 35.

87. Quale 47.

88. Quale 50.

89. Campbell, foreward to Gimbutas xiv.

90. Gimbutas xx-xxi.

91. Gimbutas 318.

92. Gimbutas 318-320.

93. McGee 66.

94. Walker 347.

95. Mary Daly, *Pure Lust: Elemental Feminist Philosophy* (Boston: Beacon Press, 1984), ix-xii.

96. McGee 67.

97. Colin Renfrew, "The Origins of Indo-European Languages," *Scientific American* 261:4 (1989), 109.

98. Renfrew 113.

99. Jean Bethke Elshtain, *Women and War* (New York: Basic Books, 1987), 171-180.

100. George L. Hart, *The Poems of Ancient Tamil: Their Milieu and Their Sanskrit Counterparts* (Berkeley: University of California Press, 1975), 108.

101. Hart 108-109.

102. Lerner 143.

103. Lerner 143.

104. Carol P. Christ, *The Laughter of Aphrodite: Reflections on a Journey to the Goddess* (San Francisco: Harper & Row, 1987), 80.

105. Julien Ries, "The Fall," in *The Encyclopedia of Religion*, ed. Mircea Eliade (New York: Macmillan, 1987), 5:256.

106. Gen. 4:8; 4:19; 4:23-24; 11:5-9.

107. Ries 265.

108. Many interpreters of this Biblical passage, of course, choose to blame Eve rather than both Adam and Eve.

109. Elizabeth Schüssler Fiorenza, "On Feminist Methodology," *Journal of Feminist Studies in Religion* 1:2 (1985), 75.

110. Holman C. Hugh, *A Handbook of Literature* (New York: Macmillan Press, 1986), 133-134.

111. Christopher Norris, "Deconstruction, Post-Modernism and the Visual Arts" in Christopher Norris & Andrew Benjamin, *What is Deconstruction?* (London: Academy Editions 1988), 15.

112. Goldenberg 41.

113. Norris and Benjamin (quoting Charles Jencks), 30.

114. Norris 12.

115. Goldenberg 42-43.

116. Goldenberg 47.

117. Goldenberg 48.

118. Goldenberg 48-49.

119. Goldenberg 47.

120. This work was first published in Russia in 1905. Subsequently, it was proven in court to be a forgery. Nevertheless, it has since been translated into many languages and reprinted dozens of times.

121. For a discussion of norms and evaluation see Mary Jo Weaver, "Who is the Goddess and Where Does She Get Us?" *Journal of Feminist Studies in Religion* 5:1 (1989), 58-59.

Contributors

Mary Gerhart
Department of Religious Studies
Hobart & William Smith College
730 S Main St.
Geneva, NY 14456
USA

Denyse Rockey
The University of Sydney
P.O. Box 1001
Potts Point
N.S.W. 2011
AUSTRALIA

Winnie Tomm
Department Coordinator
Women's Studies Program
University of Alberta
Edmonton, AB T6C 2B4
CANADA

Katherine K. Young
Faculty of Religious Studies
McGill University
3520 University St.
Montreal, PQ H3A 2A7
CANADA